Tarahumara Running Boy

My grandfather told me that Talking God comes around in the morning, knocks on the door, and says, "Get up, my grandchildren, it's time to run, run for health and wealth."

Rex Lee Jim, Navajo runner

Hopi Snake Dance Runner at Walpi

INDIAN RUNNING

NATIVE AMERICAN HISTORY & TRADITION

by
Peter Nabokov

Photographs of the
1980 Tricentennial Run
by Karl Kernberger

Ancient City Press
Santa Fe, New Mexico

Grateful acknowledgement is made to the following for permission
to quote from the works indicated:

Alfred A. Knopf: *Mornings in Mexico* by D. H. Lawrence, 1927.

Swallow Press: *The Man Who Killed The Deer* by Frank Waters, 1942.

New Mexico Magazine and Clee Woods: "Indian Track Meet,"
March, 1946.

University of California Press: *The Eastern Timbira* by Curt Nimuendaju, 1946.

Collins Publishing Co.: *The Savage and the Innocent* by David
Maybury-Lewis (World Publishing Co.), 1965.

Museum of New Mexico, *El Palacio*: "The Kick-Stick Race at
Zuni," by Roy Keech, N. 37, 1934.

Columbia University Press: *Papago Indian Religion* by Ruth
Underhill, 1946 (Papago running songs).

Wheelwright Museum of the American Indian: text of running
song from First Puberty Ceremony of Navajo Emergence Myth.

International Standard Book Number: ISBN 0-941270-41-6

Library of Congress Catalogue Number: 87-071658

First Ancient City Press printing 1987. Reprint of the edition published by Capra Press, Santa Barbara.

Cover Design
Stephen Tongier

Cover photo: Jemez runners near Zia Pueblo, 1980. Photograph by
Karl Kernberger.

Back cover photo: Courtesy of the Smithsonian Institution National
Anthropological Archives. Negative number 4660.

10   9   8   7   6   5

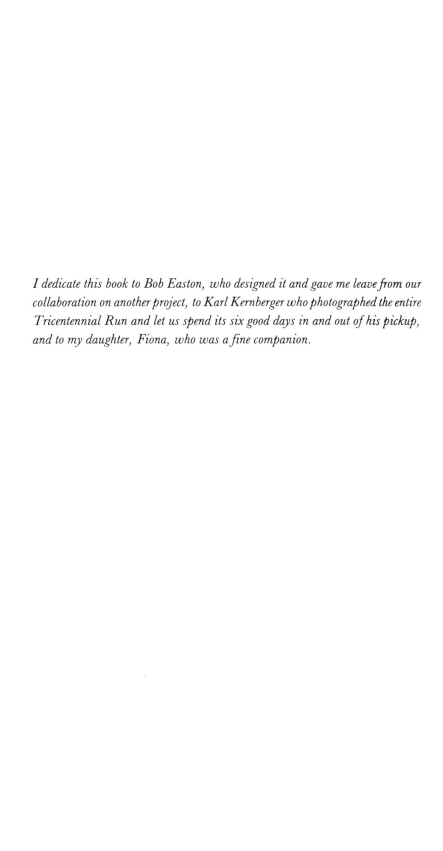

I dedicate this book to Bob Easton, who designed it and gave me leave from our collaboration on another project, to Karl Kernberger who photographed the entire Tricentennial Run and let us spend its six good days in and out of his pickup, and to my daughter, Fiona, who was a fine companion.

Contents

Petroglyph of Indian runner, Galisto Basin, New Mexico

Foreword

IN AUGUST 1980 a group of young Pueblo Indians ran over 375 miles from Taos, New Mexico to Second Mesa, Arizona. They were consecrating a milestone in their past by reenacting the courier mission, 300 years before, which had triggered the most successful Indian rebellion in American history. In this book I have tried to report that modern running event and explore the ancient roots of Indian running in the Americas. Before the coming of the white man Indians ran to communicate, fight and hunt. But, as I discovered, they also ran to enact their myths and to create a bridge between themselves and the forces of the universe.

I don't write as an advocate or a practitioner. I'm a lazy weekend runner, sometimes after work. In the adventure of preparing for this book, however, running became a loose thread in a cultural tapestry. Now I run a little more and a little differently. The experience also became an object lesson in what can happen when you track down a seemingly isolated or minimal feature of American Indian life. A whole system opens before your eyes.

This is not a scholarly treatise, nor a technical manual for non-Indian imitators, nor an official record of the Tricentennial Run. It is what happened when I covered that rare event and tugged on that cultural thread. I would like it to be an inspiration, not a handbook, for general readers interested in culture and human consciousness as well as running.

Peter Nabokov

Yuman Runner, Colorado River, 1884

1.

The World of Indian Running

OF THAT EPIC mission, this much we know.

In late spring of 1680, messengers assembled at Red Willow (Taos Pueblo) in what is today northern New Mexico. Speaking to them was a middle-aged man born in the nearby village of Grinding Stone (San Juan Pueblo). Spaniards would record him only as Popé, and revile him as "a magician," the devil incarnate. His native name, Po'pay, possibly meant "ripe squash," which could identify him as a religious leader of his village's summer moiety. With him were probably other Pueblo Indian leaders, Luis Tupatu of Picuris, Antonio Malacate of Tesuque, and his host, El Saca of Taos. They were conspiring to overthrow Spanish rule in the Southwest.

Deerskins with pictographs were handed to the runners. Po'pay told them that the uprising would come upon the new August moon, with the ripening of corn. The runners were rehearsed in the plan behind the pictographs. They were to forewarn all the seventy-odd Pueblos the Spanish had been persecuting for nearly a century, even to the Hopi villages over 300 miles away.

Word flew on foot, and August drew near. They were brought together for a second mission. Given a bundle of knotted yucca-fiber cords as countdown devices, the runners were to repeat the itinerary of Pueblos. Every village was to untie a knot each day until the cords were clear. That day they should grab hidden weapons and "burn the temples, break up the bells."

We know that information leaked out, requiring a last minute runner communiqué to push the date ahead. Two runners from Tesuque were intercepted and hanged. The revised target date: August 10. There is no description of these couriers at work, but Willa Cather's *Death Comes for the Archbishop* offers this picture of Pueblo messengers: "North of Laguna two Zuni runners sped by them, going somewhere east on 'Indian business.' They saluted Eusabio by gestures with the open palm, but did not stop. They coursed over the sand with the fleetness of young antelope, their bodies disappearing and reappearing among the sand dunes like the shadows that eagles cast in their strong, unhurried flight."

Since the Spanish had permanently settled among them in the 1590s and built their chain of missions, the Indians of these city-states had seen their lifeways disrupted and their religion defiled. Twenty years before the conspiracy was hatched at Taos, a Franciscan priest boasted of burning 1600 of their sacred kachina masks. Five years before speaking to the runners, Po'pay was among forty-seven religious men who were publicly flogged in the Santa Fe plaza.

Runners may have been organized in these Indian communities, but we know little about them. The Spaniards describe Indians on foot escaping from them on horseback. Some rituals today seem to contain trace memories of organized runners. During the corn dance at Santo Domingo in early August, for instance, messengers open the ceremony by dashing in the four cardinal directions and shortly reassembling. From east and west runners announce enemies at those frontiers, ready to raid the crops; from north and south they bring liquids to purify the warriors who must respond to this threat.

As for the use of knotted cords, the Inca developed a complicated method for recording and counting through the use of colored and knotted strings called *quipus*. The Apache had an *izze-kloth*, beaded medicine strands which some surmise were these "knotted cords," but the knotted countdown devices of California's Indians seem closer in function. The northern Maidu synchronized their funeral "burning" rite by distributing knotted cords among mourners who would untie a knot a day so as to arrive at the same time. The eastern Pomo called such cords *damálduyik*, or "day count," and did not use them for periods longer than five days; the Chemehuevi had messengers called "bringers of the knotted string." Po'pay claimed to have gotten the idea from three masked figures who told him to "make a string of yucca, tying a number of knots, as a token of the days they had to wait until they should break out." An Indian tortured by Spanish interrogators after the revolt testified: "The string was carried from village to village by the swiftest runners."

No native monuments were built to honor Po'pay or his peoples' consequent victory. Surprisingly, there is scanty mention of the major war in Indian oral tradition. Perhaps the charred shells of Catholic churches were enough, the twenty-one dead priests, the ashes of church documents, and the 380 Spaniards and Mexican Indians also killed. Superimposed on the ruins of Santa Fe's plaza, a newly-built kiva, the Indian chamber reserved for sacred activities, did symbolize the restoration of Pueblo Indian sovereignty. Over the next dozen years no Spaniards were to be found in this land. Although Don Diego de Vargas led the reconquest of the territory in 1692, Spanish control of the Indians was crippled forever. The church and the kiva have coexisted to this day. The revolt remains a victory.

Apache medicine strand

Far to the south and north of Pueblo country, details of courier-runner traditions have endured. Among peoples who developed foot messenger systems for knitting together vast territories were the Mesquakie of Iowa, the Chemehuevi of California, and the Inca of Peru. As one examines these systems it becomes clear that their runners were more than functionary athletes. They were communicators of culture; their units were absorbed into social and religious life. They were highly regarded as safekeepers of accurate information. Their status was high for they helped to keep their worlds intact and in touch.

In the 1860s a Fox runner (our name for Mesquakie) ran over 400 miles from Green Bay, Wisconsin to warn Sauk Indians along the Missouri River of an enemy attack. His name wasn't recorded but he is said to have been in his mid-fifties. He probably carried a dried buffalo heart. He was the last Mesquakie to hold the post of a'ckāpäwa, ceremonial runner.

Until the 1920s information about this courier corps was kept secret, part of Mesquakie religion to be hidden from white men's eyes. But anthropologist Truman Michelson retrieved an account of the last ceremonial runner's investiture into the brotherhood. Then he discovered references which suggested similar systems among the Sauk, Kickapoo, Menominee, Creek, Kansa, Omaha and Osage.

The Michelson document describes Mesquakie runners who lived like messenger-monks. Carrying special bowls and spoons, hosted far and wide as tribal emissaries, they alone could deliver the deciding vote in deadlocked councils. Vowing celibacy, observing strict dietary rules, promising to be truthful, they dedicated their lives to the office. In their heyday they banded in teams of three. The leader, from the Bear clan, had wind-medicine power. The member from the War Chief clan possessed deer power. The Eagle clan runner received power from the hummingbird. They were reputedly good-natured and fearless. "It was impossible for them to be unwilling," Michelson was told. "Even if they came to rivers they would cross them if they were ordered." Their very presence brought a kind of blessing. "They foresaw everything, so where these Indians had a town, (it) would be proper and not evil."

Near Shallow Water (not far from St. Louis) the Fox boy who would become the last ceremonial runner was in the thirteenth day of a fast when a hummingbird spoke to him, "Today I bless you so. You will be very fast. You will call yourself, 'ceremonial runner man.' They will send you on errands no matter how far off. So I give you (the quality of) willingness. I shall also give you the quality of tranquil braveness. You will be exactly as I am."

With the "holy gift" of speed came the power of invisibility. The hummingbird's code was strict: "You must live morally in the future." Sexual activity would despoil and weaken him. He must not jest idly with people on his mission, nor use bad words, nor steal, nor mock. Eat only turtle dove or quail, he was told, and always be clean.

For durability and power he must exchange his regular deerskin moccasins for footwear of buffalo hide. A strip of hide around his waist would remind him of his messages. He should not wear red, nor collect firewood from riverbanks where hummingbirds might be nesting. In gratitude for "this mystic power" he must burn tobacco. He must carve a special runner's bowl and spoon to use his entire life, tan a bedroll from a spotted deer's skin, and sleep on the south side of his host's *wikiup*. On runs he should carry the dried buffalo heart.

On the fourth day of instructions two hummingbirds had the boy strip down. When he was standing with the river up to his neck, they circled above his head until the earth "fell fast and whirled." The birds blew into his mouth four times, so strongly that he could not speak, as if to permanently expand his lungs for the work ahead. They said, "Perhaps this day you are the last ceremonial runner," and then they flew off.

At home the boy took a sweat bath, picked up a spotted deer hide, and soon amazed everyone by his effortless running at top speed. From village to village he delivered council declarations in record time. He burned tobacco to the forces of nature and remained clean and pure.

When he was an old man and close to death, the last runner warned: "Later on there will be many people who will ruin you.

They won't be Indians and will think nothing of your rules. Later on you will have no one who will go about telling anything that happened to you. You will have a hard time. Even whenever you die you will not know that of each other if no one goes about reporting it, when you lose the ceremonial runners.''

In the Southern California desert the Chemehuevi High Chiefs relied on a similar "ancient cult or guild" known as "The Runners," according to anthropologist Carobeth Laird. They "trotted" across their Colorado River country trails through a web of shortcuts, carrying knotted strings and messages of peace and war. They called each other "cousin" and were "lean, strong, beautiful and remarkably swift." By George Laird's time—her husband and informant—only one old-style "Runner" remained, a man named Rat Penis. He was a quiet person, smiling gently and talking little. When he ran in company, for fun, he performed like the rest. But alone he used what George Laird called "the old way."

One morning he left his friends at Cottonwood Island, in Nevada, and said he was going to the mouth of the Gila River, in southern Arizona. He didn't want anyone else along, but when he was out of sight, the others began tracking him. Beyond the nearby dunes his stride changed. The tracks "looked as if he had been 'just staggering along,' taking giant steps, his feet touching the ground at long, irregular intervals, leaving prints that became further and further apart and lighter and lighter in the sand." When they got to Fort Yuma they learned that he had arrived at sunrise of the same day he had left them. No one ever witnessed this "teleportation" technique in action. It was not done with the aid of a spirit helper, it was "ancient knowledge." He had only one friend and they called each other "sweet potato." He was not interested in women and died under the age of twenty from smallpox.

Running as a "calling" appears in other California Indian cultures. In the central region the Nomlaki "newsboys" enjoyed safe passage through enemy territory. To keep up their wind they were careful about diet and practised daily. Possibly they consumed the nutty-tasting chia seed, popular for its high nutritional value to California Indians further south. Candidates were between twenty-five and forty years of age; freed of other duties, the "newsboys" were community wards.

One named "Blind Martin" made the sixty-mile round trip between Paskenta and Tahama at night. He said he was never shot at although he conveyed news during wartime. Coming in, he would catch his breath before reciting his message word for word as he had been given it. Two people repeated it and then the issue was opened for discussion.

Another California Indian runner system, found among the Luiseño to the the south and called the *Mamish-Ahikan* ("unencumbered wind"), became the propelling motif of an elegant novel for teenagers published in 1948. The hero of Donna Preble's thoroughly researched *Yamino-Kwiti: Boy Runner of Sibi,* is torn between desiring the thrills of the courier's travelling life, following in his father's footsteps, or being groomed to become a *Pul,* or priest. Running permeates the work—couriers on trails, racing myths, children's foot races, and New Moon running rituals. Finally Yamino-Kwiti gets his wish, as he is hired as a foot messenger by the Spanish explorer, Gaspar De Portolá. We last see him, "Flying along with winged feet . . . At last he was to be a courier and see the world!"

Travellers to the lower Colorado River country returned with stories of Yuman-speaking runners. Among the Mohave in 1886, John G. Bourke heard about one Panta-cha who took less than twenty-four hours to cover nearly 200-miles from Fort Mohave to the Mohave Reservation and back. Bourke paid another Mohave two dollars for a twenty-one mile mission through heavy sand; the man made it in three and a half hours. In the same region the Cocomaricopas developed a highly regarded runner service which ultimately connected Arizona with California and Sonora, Mexico. The route was especially active toward the beginning of the nineteenth century, as Cocomaricopas and Halchidhomas carried news between San Gabriel, Mexico, Tucson and San Diego. Yuman runners were prized for the two qualities which all runner systems regarded as critical, "endurance and reliability."

In the east the Iroquois Confederacy was able to dominate upper New York State in part because of its organized runners. They ran on the 240-mile "Iroquois Trail" which bound together the Confederacy, requiring seventy hours to cover the country between the "eastern door" of the Mohawk, near present-day Albany, to the "western door" of the Seneca, near Buffalo. The Quaker James Emlen records in his 1794 journal that one of Chief Cornplanter's runners, Sharp Shins, did the ninety rolling miles from Canadaigua to Niagra between sunrise and sunset. To sustain themselves the runners nibbled scorched cornmeal. They carried beaded "wampum belts" to summon mourners when a chief died. When Seneca runners entered races, they might also steep Toad Rush in water, then drink it as an emetic three times during the week prior to the meet; they also dieted on sweet milk and Indian corn bread.

Like the Inca of Peru, the Iroquois used their runners in relays to increase range and efficiency. During the Revolutionary War, one runner left Tonawanda at daybreak to get word to Avon, forty miles away, and returned by noon. Dispatched usually in pairs, they "took their way through the forest, one behind the other, in perfect silence," according to Lewis Henry Morgan. When night fell, they navigated by the stars, using the Pleiades in fall and winter, their Loon constellation in spring and summer.

These runner-systems were in action across North and South American lands which had been discovered, named, and traversed long before the white man appeared. Trails and throughfares led everywhere, allowing goods from Hudson Bay ultimately to reach the Gulf of Mexico. Messengers, porters and traders kept aboriginal America busy with goods and ideas. New information about pre-Columbian trade networks comes to light each year. In the Southwest archeologists using sophisticated "remote sensing" equipment are surveying a pre-historic road system in New Mexico's Chaco Canyon with some 200 miles of curbed roadways, sometimes displaying staircases over bluffs. We know that the Maya of Yucatan laid roads, known as *sacbe*, of white limestone; by way of them runners and porters linked up market and ceremonial centers in the jungle.

Spanish writers refer to seasoned runners among the Aztec of Mexico "who could run like the wind." Ceremonially they served to disperse fire from a sacred flame periodically rekindled in a central temple; functionally, they moved in relays to convey messages. *Correos* to the Spanish, *titlantil* to the Aztec, they were valued for veracity as well as strength. The historian William H. Prescott says that these men, "trained from childhood," covered one to two hundred miles a day, bearing hides covered with hieroglyphic writing. Hernán Cortés wrote that within twenty-four hours of his landing at Chianiztlan in May 1519, runners had described to Montezuma, 260 miles away, his ships, men, guns and horses. Prescott's most quoted item concerns runners who managed to supply Montezuma's kitchen with fresh fish from the Gulf of Mexico.

Inca chasqui *runner.*

By far the greatest pre-Columbian road system ran over 2,500 miles from northern Ecuador to southern Chile. The Inca highway carried the most institutionalized of all runner organizations, the *chasquis*—meaning "to exchange." This combination of road construction and courier administration produced a communications network of runners equal to those found in Rome, Persia and China. The coastal stretch covered some 1,100 miles, and featured molded curbing, retaining walls where they cut through hills, and fruit trees along the shoulder. Wrinkling along the spine of the Andes, the highland road was narrower and more engineered with causeways and culverts. From both highways arteries branched east, north and south to connect the Incan capital with the "Four Quarters of the World."

Although the *chasqui* system of runners as the Spanish knew it was developed in the mid-15th century by the Ninth Inca, Pachacuti Inca Yupanqui, before this floresence of functional running earlier running complexes or rituals probably existed in Peru. On the pottery of the Mochica, a coastal culture which antedated the Inca by six or seven centuries, drawings seem to depict costumed runners. In one outstretched hand they carry bags, and bean-like design motifs suggest a pre-*quipu* device for keeping track of messages. It has also been suggested that the Nazca lines, great paths straight as rulers scratched into the Peruvian plains, were race tracks similar to those hacked from the Brazilian jungle for Indian "log-runners."

By the reign of the Eleventh Inca, Huayna Capac (1493-1528), the *chasqui* system of trails and post stations had been perfected. Every half league or so on major roads pairs of oven-shaped stone shelters, called *c'oklya*, were manned by waiting runners who kept their eyes ready for a bobbing white feather, the telltale bonnet of the *chasqui*. Forewarned by the approaching man's blast on a conch shell trumpet, they listened for the message he yelled ahead. The incoming runner might also hand over a colored and knotted *quipu* message. At top speed the fresh relayer would dash about two miles to the next station.

Chasquis were drawn from high-born families, selected for their devotion and bound to secrecy. They worked fifteen-day shifts and were supported by local tax. Their "news center" was Cuzco, the "Navel of the World" and seat of the Incan empire. Within two or three hours, word of a local rebellion could be delivered 500 to 600 leagues away. Based on times recorded during the civil wars following Spanish conquest, word travelled about 150 miles a day. While the Spanish horse-mail took twelve to thirteen days from Lima to Cuzco, runners could cover the distance in three. It was said that a snail picked from a leaf at Tumi, in the far north of the empire, could be delivered alive to Cuzco, in the southern highlands.

Once the Spaniards recognized the utility of the *chasqui* system they retained a modified version; in the colonial period one chronicler, Poma de Ayala, argued that the service of runners was so vital they deserved the same salary as mayors.

In North America the last accounts of runner-messengers tend to focus on the Hopi. "For a dollar," wrote George Wharton James in 1903, "I have several times engaged a young man to take a message from Oraibi to Keam's Canyon, a distance of seventy-two miles,

Running Pueblo clown and turkey

and he has run on foot the entire distance, delivered his message, and brought me an answer within thirty-six hours."

When it came to communicating with the railhead, local army officers preferred Hopis over their own horsemen. Walter Hough describes a Hopi leaving Oraibi Pueblo at 4:00 in the afternoon and delivering his message at midnight in Winslow. This was sixty-five miles at night over unfamiliar ground; then he turned around and ran home. Edward S. Curtis has his story: a Hopi named Letayu carried a note from Keams Canyon to Fort Wingate in two days, spending the first night at Fort Defiance. The third morning on his return he left Wingate before "gray dawn," got to Defiance before sunrise, and arrived in Keams Canyon that afternoon—over 200 miles in three days.

When Charlie Talawepi of Old Oraibi died two years ago his grandson, Roy Albert, believes he was a century old. Talawepi must have been about thirty when he was summoned by the local Indian agent at Tuba City, Walter Runke, Sr. Renegades on the Navajo reservation were causing trouble; he had to contact Flagstaff immediately.

"My grandad set out about three in the morning, sort of alternating sprinting and jogging," as Albert told me the story. "Some place between Cameron and Grey Mountain he saw the sun hit the San Francisco Peaks. He piled up rocks there to remember how far he'd come. About forty miles from Flagstaff, at the springs near Lone Pine, he rested again, dipping his piki bread into some water and eating, but not too much.

"It must have been about noon when he got to Flag and went right to the Babbitt Brothers Trading Post. The people there just sort of shook their heads. I guess he handed them the message and they wired it to the Bureau of Indian Affairs people in Washington. He only stayed a half-hour. They rubbed him down. Before he took off they tied food packs around his waist. But they were too heavy so he let them fall off, just keeping his water flask.

"On the way back," Albert said, "he kept changing his gait. As he was coming from Cameron his legs began tightening up. Five or six miles from Moenkopi he walked some. Then he ran. When he came within a mile of the village he was so tired he could only walk. He got in around ten or eleven that night. It was the longest run he ever made, but he didn't think it was a big deal. He felt it for days afterward though. They figure he'd gone 156 miles in less than twenty-four hours. Agent Runke gave him a twenty-dollar silver piece.''

Gods and animals ran long before Indian men and women ever did. Thereafter the gods told people to do it, and the animals showed them how. ''There is nothing that Indians like so well as to run races,'' a Zuni Indian told Anna Risser. ''Maybe that is because the gods in the far past settled so many difficult questions by races.'' In practically every tribe's oral history, running folklore instructed and entertained. Mythic races helped to order the world as we know it, providing a model and mandate for the activity which human beings would perpetuate. Racing contests decided the first temperaments and physical characteristics of animals, and played a part in allocating their territories and status in the emerging world. Often these creatures were themselves clan originators, whose groupings would then be mirrored by man's social organization.

The Cheyenne tell of the mythic race which decisively separated men from animals. In the time when men and animals could converse, the fast, split-hooved rallied for a Great Race against men and their helpers, from Devil's Tower, North Dakota to Wyoming's Grand Tetons. In the relays, men were paired against elk, dog against deer, eagle against antelope, hawk against buffalo. The last lap saw hawk pull away to alight on the highest peak, with buffalo spent at the bottom. The split-hooved creatures withdrew without a word, thereafter eternal losers in men's hunts. This began the naming of the bravest Cheyenne warriors—Hawk soldiers.

Some of these Genesis stories have foot races creating pieces of the outer cosmos and local topography. To a number of California Indian tribes, the Milky Way emerged from such races, either as ''dust'' kicked up in the race between Coyote and Wildcat (Cahuilla), or as the ''tracks'' of Deer and Antelope in their six-day

Crow runners: (l. to r.) Sees-the-Ground, Pretty Paint, Comes-Up-Red, Victory Singer

race (Tachi Yokuts). In some Southwestern ceremonies lies the hint that four such primoridal runs created the seasons and cardinal directions, echoing the Mayan myth which describes the unfolding of the tangible world behind the "marching" about of a First Man figure. In California Indian mythology the Sun once ran. When Coyote bested him, the world became dark until Wood Duck revived him. Local geography could originate from mythic runs; the Yokuts say the Sacramento River was born out of a runner moving inland, the river evolving in his wake.

Down-to-earth fables used the context of the race to poke fun and entertain while teaching appropriate behavior and morality as their sub-texts. The Cheyenne, Atsina, Dakota, Assiniboine, Blackfoot and San Carlos Apache tell how an Old Man character, having tricked some plump baby rabbits onto his cooking coals, loses the meal through a challenge to race by trickster Coyote. Coyote appears crippled as he limps toward the turn-around marker with Old Man enjoying a confident lead. But on the home stretch he opens up, and Old Man puffs into camp to discover Coyote sucking the last rabbit bone. Moral: the race was as fair as Old Man's treatment of the rabbits.

Other tales seem to function as chalk talks, teaching runners how to measure their stride and energy, use their heads, and seek spiritual assistance. They commonly pit slower animals, like Turtle or Crane, against swifter beasts to emphasize the skills of pacing and cleverness. Southeastern people like the Alabama and Creek tell of proud Hummingbird being challenged by Crane to race. Overly confident, Hummingbird zips ahead in daylight, but stops to sleep at night, while Crane flaps patiently along. On the final evening, to avoid waking Hummingbird, Crane heads for higher altitudes, reaches the ocean, and wins the right to inhabit the marshlands forever. The lesson: racing is as much an exercise of consciousness as of speed.

Stories of racing trickery also set the precedent for human beings to use magic to ensure success. The Shoshoneans tell how Frog beat Wolf. Wolf never figures out that his opponent is actually a conspiracy of identical animals, who always pop into view a length ahead of him. For both the Mono of California and the Navajo, a Frog runner urinates on the track to blind or bewitch his opposition.

These stories became directives to run and race as the old related them to the young. They also supported the notion that running could be a link between worlds, a way of communicating with timeless spirits and powers. For some Indian peoples, it was as if running became a sort of sign language. This was Alexander M. Stephen's impression, after he was told by a Hopi: "When the sand Chief takes the prayer feathers, to pray on them and leave them in the fields, he goes barefooted and without covering on limbs or body, that the Cloud chiefs may see he wants rain. He runs swiftly that the clouds may come swiftly, that his prayers be quickly answered.

"He loosens his hair, and lets it hang over his shoulders, for thus the Cloud chiefs carry the rain clouds. He makes a far circuit on the first day, because the Cloud chiefs live far away. He goes to the northwest, southwest, northeast, and southeast, to call the attention of all the cloud chiefs . . . on each succeeding day, he travels in a shorter radius. It is thus we want the rain clouds to come, nearer and nearer, until on the concluding day of the ceremony they shall have come overhead and poured down the heavy rain upon ourselves, our houses and all the surrounding lands, and we may see the arroyo full of running water and listen to its sweet sound."

Anthropology labels such action-prayers "sympathetic magic," suggesting a causal relationship, a separation between actors and the elements they seek to influence. But in the case of Indian running, at least, this fails to convey a participatory dimension to the experience.

Among the Navajo, for instance, running meant joining in the motion which is at the heart of life itself. Their Genesis is called "moving upward;" everything from the Navajo settlement pattern to healing rituals contains the motif of ceaseless motion. Writes Margot Astrov: "No other mythology has been fertile in inventing vehicles of speed and efficient transfer as that of the Navajo." This positive identification between running, motion and the life force becomes incarnate in Pueblo ceremonial running.

While the Hopi or Tewa who "runs for rain" is enacting his people's desire for what they would like to happen—running outside of the message he carries—he also seems to undergo a deeper transformation. He is performing Aristotle's definition of motion as "the mode in which the future belongs to the present. . .the joint presence of potentiality and actuality.''

He does more than run "like the wind," for that metaphor distances him from the element and the experience. To some degree he turns into rain-cloud-blown-by-wind, or sun-on-his-path. His running is a deed done for effect later as well as, in Lucien Lévy-Bruhl's phrase, a mystical participation "independent of time and space."

The runner becomes his message.

Hopi tradition provides us with a few glimpses of the 1680 Revolt. At Oraibi two warriors named Haneeya and Chavayo charged through the church to kill friars Jose de Espeleta and Agustin de Santa Maria in their quarters. After the fighting, Shipaulovi village says that a pregnant woman of the Bear Clan was escorted away from the violence-contaminated town to a place of refuge for bearing children. When her child was twenty days old, he was presented to the sun according to Hopi custom. This symbolized the rebirth of a free Hopi people, and the return of peace.

As 1980 drew near, the Hopi claim this legend guided their decision to make rebirth, reaffirmation and reassessment the themes of their own Tricentennial. To the east, along the Rio Grande, Herman Agoyo, the forty-six-year-old executive director of the Eight Northern Pueblos, had been wondering for a year how to mark the Revolt's anniversary. Since boyhood he and Alfonso Ortiz had shared their pride in hailing from Po'pay's home village of San Juan.

"I know now," says Agoyo, "that this concern sparked the dreams I experienced at the time. In these dreams I saw myself meeting and talking with people. The details of these interactions were never clear in my dreams, but I knew they were about the Tricentennial.'' By mid-1979 Hopi planning had crystalized around the symbolic run from Taos, while the eastern Pueblos represented by Agoyo were concentrating on their annual Po'pay race and Arts and Crafts Fair to honor the revolt; but by fall both were discussing joint participation in a reenactment of the 1680 courier mission.

Planning was not smooth. To this day the twenty-six surviving Pueblo villages place high value on their individual autonomy. They do share a background as sedentary agriculturalists who live in compact stone-and-adobe villages with similar ceremonial patterns. But they represent six different languages, their attitudes toward progress and tradition vary widely, and they cling too proudly to their separate histories and identity to be railroaded into unanimity. Po'pay probably had a hard time getting them to agree, and three centuries later it was more difficult. Alfonso Ortiz hoped the celebration would be a chance to ''let us celebrate our distinctiveness,'' but that distinctiveness held subtle cracks. Only rumors came from the closed door meetings, but the Hopis were reportedly adamant about running the whole distance, while Santo Domingo Pueblo, it was said, objected to any Hopi participation, claiming they weren't true Pueblos; their purists also wanted the run to be on Indian paths and in moccasins.

As it was, all wore sneakers and the Hopi running machine played the most prominent role. Santo Domingo pulled out its runners. As the event loomed, Herman Agoyo arranged for the printing and stitching of leather pouches, each to contain a symbolic piece of double-knotted rawhide and messages which read:

FATHER SUN WE RUN FOR YOU AS WE DID 300 YEARS AGO—WITH YOUR BLESSING FOR OUR PEOPLE. AND ALL CREATIONS YOU HAVE GIVEN. MEET AT SANTO DOMINGO PUEBLO AUGUST 9, 1980.

At this meeting the Pueblos were to receive from an emissary of the Spanish government silver-headed canes of office to add to those the New Mexico Pueblos had acquired in the 17th century from Spain, and in the 19th century from President Lincoln. They symbolized the continuous affirmation of their sovereignty. But the

29

Hopi Basket Dance Racers, 1919

message was odd, since Santo Domingo runners weren't involved, the Hopis had never been part of the cane symbolism, and the gathering was slated for the day before the Hopis even delivered their message home.

No matter to the Hopi, since they conceived of their run as a somewhat separate event from the start, and were also the only tribe to be savoring a fairly clear-cut military victory; they were not re-Christianized when Spaniards swept back into the region after 1692.

As I talked with the Hopi painter Fred Kabotie in Santa Cruz and Professor of Anthropology Alfonso Ortiz in Santa Fe in late winter, 1980, I started to wonder, what was this event which seems to be emerging from the union of Indian ceremony and white man's commemoration? Since 1792 one ritual drama had already become central to New Mexico's historical image; ironically, the annual Santa Fe Fiesta celebrated the reversal of the All-Pueblo Revolt. Its centerpiece was a twenty-eight-inch sculpture of the Madonna which, went the story, had miraculously escaped the torches of Indian rebels. Every August it was paraded through the state capital streets, and historical personages enacted by prominent citizens reaffirmed the Hispanic religious, ethnic and civic identity.

This Tricentennial seemed almost a symbolic rejoinder, except that it was a one-shot affair and quietly planned, largely for Indian consumption. In the Pueblo world there was no precedent for self-conscious creation of public ritual to sanctify historical events. The religious, ethnic and civic features of their world-view were indivisibly renewed with each season's rites according to a format handed down from the Gods. If these tribes were attempting to retool the white man's "calling to mind" (commemoration) that helped explain the improvisational unfolding of the event.

Some of its symbols were still unborn. Agoyo was supervising the distribution of the sackful of pouches, but they did not possess the same meaning and mana for all. Kabotie was wondering how the Hopi steering committee would figure out the logistics. "Somebody must have brought in the knotted strings," he told me, "but nobody remembers, there aren't any legends. . . . The rebellion took place on the same day. In my village of Shungopovi they killed the priests

31

and his associates, as at Oraibi and Awatovi. . . . We are working it out so the runner who carries the knotted string can come into the Hopi villages on time.''

Backed by grants from the New Mexico Humanities Council and the National Endowment for the Humanities, Agoyo's own planning committee began to see the fruit of their labors. The Po'pay foot races and Arts Festival held on July 18–20 at San Juan were a great success; well-known local runners Steve Gachupin, Al Waquie, Tony Sandoval, and Bill Pangakos were in attendance. The U.S. Post Office approved a special postmark, to be issued August 14-15 at San Juan Pueblo and Albuquerque, depicting the Tricentennial logo of Po'pay's two legendary runners from Tesuque. Everyone realized the upcoming run was becoming more than a social event, yet seemed to trust that its deeper importance and symbolism would emerge in its doing rather than any interpretation before the fact.

When I flew to New Mexico in early August to cover the run for *New Mexico* and *Rocky Mountain* magazines with photographer Karl Kernberger and my daughter, Fiona, I knew little of this background, but I had some hunches and hopes. I expected no mystery in its outcome; this was a happening, not a competition. It could offer an unusual entrée into what anthropologist Leslie White once termed the ''cultural quarantine'' of these tribes, whose insular and self-protective communities have remained impressively resistant to outside investigation. During most ritual occasions cameras and even notepads are prohibited; we were allowed both. I would not abuse my welcome and planned to research background on running traditions after I got home.

As Karl picked me up in Santa Fe at 3:30 in the morning on August 5th, I expected the experience to feature a piece of Pueblo history replayed. I also hoped it would move me a little closer towards understanding how running had helped to keep Indian cultures alive.

Hopi Bear Clan racer

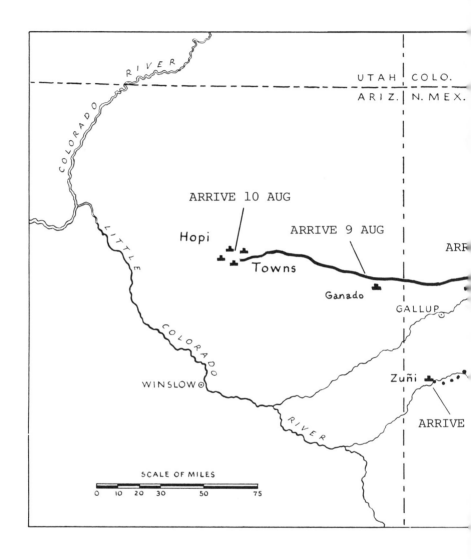

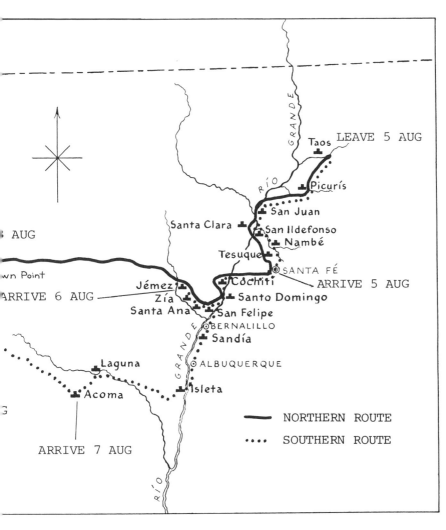

Routes of the Tricentennial run, August 1980, commemorating the 1680 All-Pueblo Revolt (adapted from Bird's Eye View of the Pueblos *by Stanley S. Stubbs. Copyright ©1950 by the University of Oklahoma).*

Runners leaving Taos, 5 August 1980
(photograph by Sam Bingham)

2.

Taos to Santa Fe
5 August

I WANT TO have a look at the Taos Pueblo relay race track. On ethnographic maps it runs before the turquoise-painted doorways of the North Side house block and carries east for a half mile, toward the mountain pass which opened the Pueblo to influences from the plains tribes.

But this 5:00 a.m., as our green pickup creeps between the toll booth and San Geronimo church, the mist is heavy following a recent heat wave. Inside Taos' melting adobe wall, where electricity is banned, the picture postcard architecture seems swallowed up. I hear only the gurgling of Taos Creek bisecting the earthen plaza, the artery tying Taos to its main shrine, Blue Lake, twenty miles north in the dark green mass of 12,282-foot Taos Mountain.

Even in broad daylight the sunken path of the relay track would probably have escaped me. These east-to-west racing stretches of the Tiwa- and Tewa-speaking Pueblos are marked only by inconspicuous boulders, yet they belong to the civic precincts which distinguish their way of life from the nation surrounding them. ''We are in one nest,'' goes a Taos saying. Tampering with the race track alignment would draw an instant outcry. When the 2.8 mile road we had just driven was first surveyed in the mid-1950s, from the town of Taos to the Pueblo, the Indians claimed an ancient foot-racing track would be violated, and fought its construction for years.

Fifteen minutes later idling cars and pickups form a gauntlet in the North Plaza. A series of vans sweep in, emptying about forty Hopi runners. Culturally their Arizona world is nearly as removed from Taos as is Ireland from Wales. These young men have signed up blind for this once-in-a-lifetime *nana'mü'-nawa*. Part of the word, stenciled on the rear window of the blue Hopi Emergency Medical Treatment van, describes ''a water course flowing with water''—the desired result of so much Hopi ritual running. It has brought these runners over 300 miles, and they look dazed after three hours sleep on the hardwood floors of Taos day school gym.

Cowled like Arabs in their flannel sheeting, two Taos elders bless their runners with water from the stream running through the plaza. Townfolk hurry to watch from the bank. Headlights from incoming cars strobe their backs, another wall protecting a Taos moment from prying eyes. As the shivering boys rejoin the crowd, their breath is fogged, their somber faces drip with holy water.

The Hopis huddle around a young man with shoulder-length hair, Manchurian mustache and cocky bearing. He is Bruce Hamana, a twenty-year-old, part-time rock guitarist from Hotevilla. A Bear Clan member, at this moment he assumes a leadership role he will hold through the return home six days away. ''Have good heart,'' he cheers the boys. Around him growling engines, flashing headlights, milling supporters and signs of dawn are making his runners impatient.

''We're running for the people,'' Hamana's voice cracks with emotion. ''It goes beyond athletics. This might not be done for another 300 years. Turn around and shake the hand of your brother. This is more than a race. It means something.''

Nearby Bruce Gomez sheds warm-up pants and kicks stiffness out of his legs. Twenty-two years old, he is regarded as one of Taos' promising young men. A track runner since thirteen, he has coached Taos' youth programs and earlier this summer organized the local "Fun Run." His grandfather was the Taos notable Geronimo "Standing Buffalo" Gomez. He is a natural to stand in for the messenger to whom Po'pay entrusted the first knotted cord. With other Taos boys he crowds around John Concha and Joe Sun-Hawk Sandoval, Taos traditionalists, who intone a last-minute blessing as if sending them off to war.

Darting into the area drenched by car lights, a Hopi with hair to his waist strews a holy corn meal "road" on the beaten ground—an ancient and universal Pueblo rite "opening" and blessing the route ahead. All Hopis, drivers of support vehicles as well as runners, instinctively queue up and trip across it, prefiguring and sanctifying the journey to come. It is 5:20 a.m. Gomez takes his pouch. Patrick Secakuku and Louis Josytewa claim the one destined for Hopi. A glance of agreement, and they are moving fast.

Within a stone's throw appears the stepped "cloud" facade of San Geronimo Church, built in 1848 long after the Indians put the old one to the torch. The runners hurtle past it, a honking train of well-wishers in hot pursuit.

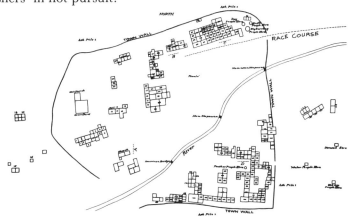

Taos Pueblo, showing relay track

Traditionally Taos runners turn out for relay races as part of annual feast days, September 30th (El Dia de San Geronimo) and May 3rd (El Dia de Santa Cruz). Long the Tahiti of the Southwest to white painters and writers, Taos, and its races, have inspired much interpretive prose. The Indians haven't explained much on their own; Taos is notoriously close-mouthed about its rituals despite a century of efforts to penetrate them. The racing appears associated with the sun, the runners through their exertion strengthening its movement across the sky. In the Tiwa-speaking towns of Taos and Picuris, as well as the six Tewa-speaking towns further down the Rio Grande, "sun road" race tracks on the earth reflect the route of that heavenly body. Alfonso Ortiz points out that these races seem to occur at "actual or culturally construed changes of season." At such periods of major shift in social patterns, the competitiveness actually serves to strengthen community bonds as divisions within the villages run side by side for cosmic regeneration.

Taos' two divisions, the North and South Side kiva groups, are pitted against each other in these races. (Outsiders have been told this helps to select the following year's officialdom but that may be an Indian way to be polite and protect the truth.) Early on race day, medicine men exorcise the track from sorcery by either side. As the running gets underway, outsiders are often confused by the jumble of footmen. Both teams have men stationed at either end of the track. Starting from the east, two runners break for the west end to tag their partners. Back and forth this continues until one side gains an entire lap. In the old days their hair was braided, bells jangled at their waists, tufts of eagle down dotted their bodies to keep them light. While the breechcloths of racers whipped the air, runners in line had their legs grazed by older men with large eagle feathers to impart power.

Later, writer Tracy McCallum kindly sent me his eye-witness account of the September 1980 relays: "Their ages must have varied from four-year-olds to eighty-year-olds. Teles 'Good Morning' Reyna, a man in his eighties, ran a lap. I was at the west end of the course and, at about the middle of the race, a young fellow was just

about to come to the finish line when one of the whippers (race atten-
dants) reached out with an aspen branch to swat him for being slow.
The fellow swerved to avoid the blow and tripped over his own feet,
falling head over heels. A great roar of sympathy came out of the
crowd of spectators and the whipper crossed over the line to help him
back up. He was mildly injured but the whipper and others made a
great fuss over him and helped him away. It makes sense that they
would both spur him on and care for him during the mishap, since
each runner represents the welfare of the entire tribe.''

Taos also featured the "world around" long distance race. From
their relay track's western end, three or four young men would head
north, running ten to fifteen miles by the January full moon, praying
to the stars and the moon for courage and strength. Anthropologist
Elsie Clews Parsons heard that "world around" runs led to a mountain shrine called "where-the-stone-men-are" where runners left
pollen, cornmeal, and turkey and eagle feather offerings with
prayers for long life. It is difficult to find out whether these runs are
still performed; one grows hesitant about passing on epitaphs to
American Indian ritual, not from sentimentality, but because often
one is simply wrong.

In Taos mythology a "world around" race between Turquoise
Boy and Deer fixed the supremacy of hunters over game, and taught
why it is wise to exorcise your race track. Grandmother Gopher
bewitched the trail which passes through a legendary site called
Coyote Ears House, lifts to Taos Peak, and finally reaches Fog
House near the saddle overlooking Blue Lake. Soon after Turquoise
Boy and Deer took off, Turquoise Boy spat out some of Grand-
mother Gopher's magic potion, whereupon gopher holes tripped
Deer up. Later he spat again, and berry bushes lured Deer to nibble.
As the fog lifted above Blue Lake, the waiting throng noticed Tur-
quoise Boy streaking in front, with Deer limping behind.

In another story Deer Boys win out. It is well after Creation;
Taos Pueblo is begging animals for salvation from a plague of witches. Deer Woman schedules a "world around" race—in some versions five times around a mountain. Deer Boys must vie against two

skin-covered skeletons, witches who transform into swift falcons. The Deer Boys chew five herbs which they spit in the four directions, causing a downpour which waterlogs the falcons' feathers. As Deer Boys finish ahead of the birds, the people club to death every sorcerer save one who pleads for mercy. For their generosity Taos still must live under the threat of witchcraft. In the San Ildefonso Pueblo variant, Antelope's medicine helps him win in a contest around the Pueblo's sacred mountain, and the event explains the creation of snakes.

Some Taos running tales establish animal characteristics. Deer agreed to run against Antelope so long as they followed their run around Taos Mountain by a climb over its rocky summit. Antelope's horns are wagered against Deer's dew claws. With lengthy strides Antelope easily triumphs over Deer on level ground. In the high country, however, Deer bounds past her through the pine-covered slopes. That is why both animals have antlers, but only Deer shows dew claws above her hooves. (In an Apache version, Deer is given Antelope's hip fat.)

Taos folklore provides its listeners with an incentive to run. Writers who have found the village's races an irresistible inspiration carry them beyond this tribal context. On September 30, 1922, Mable Dodge Luhan, the queen of Taos' Bohemian set, brought a tall guest with a red beard to San Geronimo Day. Among the cowboys and sinewy Navajos D. H. Lawrence looked amusing; an ill-fitting grey suit on his thin frame, a ten-gallon Stetson pulled down over his ears. But his antennae were aquiver with impressions. In the essay, *Indians and Entertainment*, Lawrence says the celebrations illustrated how "The Indian way of consciousness is different from and fatal to the Indian. The two ways, the two streams, are never to be united. They are not even to be reconciled. There is no bridge, no canal of connexion. . . ."

In the next sentence, as if this insight were a dare to his literary powers, Lawrence tried to create that "canal of connexion" and committed the sin of romanticism his essay railed against:

> You can see this so plainly in the Indian races. Naked and daubed with clay to hide the nakedness, and to take the anoint-

ment of the earth; stuck over with bits of fluff of eagle's down, to be anointed with the power of the air, the youths and men whirl down the racing track in relays. They are not racing to win a race. They are not racing for a prize. They are not racing to show their prowess.

They are putting forth all their might, all their strength, in a tension that is half anguish, half ecstasy, in the effort to gather into their souls more and more of the creative fire, the creative energy which will carry their tribe through the year, through the vicissitudes of the months. . . . As if hurled from a catapult, the Indian throws himself along the course, working his body strangely, incomprehensibly. And when his turn comes again, he hurls himself forward with greater intensity, to greater speed, driving himself, as it were, into the heart of the fire. And the old men along the track encourage him, urge him with their green twigs. . . . And he walks away at last, his chest lifting and falling heavily, a strange look in his eyes, having run with the changeless god who will give us nothing unless we overtake him.

To novelists N. Scott Momaday and Frank Waters the cameo of the Indian runner flying across the landscape solved a problem with dramatizing Indian life. Novels generally hook on individuals and crises, but authentic fiction about Indians is hard put to lift individuals from the clutches of their culture. Few creative imaginations stretch beyond the repeated theme of the native rebel who eventually returns to his ethos. Where their protagonist is running, however, otherwise untenable motivations and inferences become valid. The extreme—anathema to the tribal ideal which seeks stability like a gyroscope—becomes acceptable. The Indian of reality almost fuses with the Indian of fantasy, running ''like the wind,'' one with earth and sky. The novelist can adapt this riveting image to convey the man of torn identity, running towards choice, resolution, reaffirmation, peak experience, without unduly stretching the facts.

Nor were anthropologists immune to the image's attraction. Alexander M. Stephen described Hopi runners as ''highly poetic.'' After witnessing part of the morning runs at Jemez, the men ''hallooing'' as they appeared, freshly-washed hair flowing behind them, Elsie Clews Parsons wrote, ''this early morning rite is a picture never to be forgotten.'' It is the same scene N. Scott Momaday made central to his Pulitzer Prize-winning novel, *House Made of*

Taos relay runners, 1893

Dawn, also drawn from Jemez tradition: "He was alone and running on. All of his being was concentrated in the sheer motion of running on, and he was past caring about the pain. Pure exhaustion laid hold of his mind, and he could see at last without having to think. He could see the rain and the rivers and the fields beyond. He could see the dark hills at dawn. He was running, and under his breath he began to sing."

Toward the close of his novel *The Man Who Killed the Deer* Frank Waters has his hero, Martiniano, enter the lists for the Taos relay race. Until now Waters has skillfully balanced the profile of community as protagonist with the tale of Martiniano's identity crisis. Using the race to celebrate his hero's psychic homecoming, Waters gets as carried away as Lawrence. Martiniano's testing of his physical limits represents the war he's been waging within himself. His running also signifies his surrender of individuality, as he rushes into the cyclical rhythms of his native world. It works because for once those rhythms sanction drama, stress, urgency and ecstatic participation.

It was a beautiful May morning when he took his place in line. Palemon had helped to paint him. His body was bare save for a colored scarf wrapped round his loins for a breech-clout, streaked with gray clay and stripes of red and yellow. His hair was gathered in a knot, plastered tight and stuck with tufts of eagle-down. He wore no moccasins, but around his ankles were tied strings of fur. The wide, dusty race track, immemorially worn down below the level of fields and sage-plain, ran east and west, the way the sun travels. It led from a quarter of a mile beyond the town into the breach of broken wall, past a kiva, and across the plaza along the south pyramid of the pueblo. The terraced walls quivered with color in the bright sunshine, a solid blanket of spectators. The plaza was filling with more visitors. And up and down the long, stone-pitted course the old men paraded with their green branches keeping back the crowd.

At the far end of the track around Martiniano waited one group of racers. Fifty men and boys or more, all painted, plastered and bedaubed. And at the far end, against a jutting pueblo wall, waited the other group. Suddenly, at a signal, the first two runners started. Relay fashion, they hurtled down the track, heads up, straining forward like two hounds. To release at the far end two others who came stumbling and panting back up the course.

So it kept up under the brilliant climbing sun, between the shouting visitors and the silent, blanketed throng. Two naked boys down and two back. Whipped along by the old men with their green branches, their anxious shouts. Bruised feet, a stumble on a protruding stone. A boy, sick with over-exertion, vomiting in the brush. Then an old man kneading his belly with curative fingers, and pushing him back into line for yet another effort.

There have always been races. The long distance races in the old days when young men ran fifteen, twenty miles through the snowy mountains—the race around the world. And still there are the shorter spring and fall races. They are the valiant expenditures of man's puny efforts and unfaltering courage to meet and run forward with the everlasting wonder of creation.

45

And so, one after another, the young men hurtled forward over the stones with bare, bruised feet; with naked bodies painted red and yellow, black and gray; with their plastered hair stuck full of tufts of eagle-down to catch the power of air. Running not to win from one another, but extending all their strength to the sun for his new race, that once again he might return it to them, the creative power to carry the tribe forward another year. Running in panting bursts of speed while the old men along the track urged them along still faster with their green branches, their wavering, anxious shouts of encouragement. "Oom-a-pah! Oom-a-pah!"

It is a race of the individual against the limits of his own flesh, and it is the unending race of all humanity with the wonder of creation. No man wins. No man loses. But as each walks away, his broad chest heaving, his knees trembling, it is with the ecstatic look in his eyes of one who has spent himself to the full and, before he faltered, seen over the horizon the sunrise glow of his final victory.

Relayers at east end of Taos race track

While literary figures have tried to capture the spirit of the Taos relay race in word, another people, also alien to the Pueblo world, adopted it in deed, layering on even richer symbolism. It isn't clear when exactly the Athabaskan-speaking Navajo and Apache first entered Pueblo land, but the branch known as the Jicarilla Apache probably became neighbors to Taos soon after 1500 A.D. There are stories that in the mid-17th century some Taoseños, restive under Catholic oppression, lived among the plains-dwelling Jicarilla for some years. Shortly after the Apaches first witnessed the races, they seemed to have seized upon them as a chance to celebrate in one festival their new residency and identity.

In the mid-1930s, when anthropologist Morris Opler visited the Jicarilla, the event not only betrayed Taos elements but also touches of Tewa racing customs from down river. Elevated from a subsidiary ritual, it now climaxed the three-day Jicarilla festival held on San Antonio Day—September 15.

The Apaches told Opler that their relays started with a cosmic "world around" run in which Moon had gambled the fruits of the earth against Sun's animal kingdom. As these celestial chiefs competed through a four-year race cycle—perhaps creating a new season each meet—they alternately won "to insure both kinds of food for mankind." When the moon triumphed, it meant good farming; the sun's victory promised good hunting. Passing on the custom to the first Apaches, they warned: Stop this ceremony and you starve.

Opposing teams are drawn from the two divisions of Jicarilla society, eastern *Llanero* people, who identify with the plains and run for the moon, and *Ollero* or "mountain people," whose standard is the sun. As at Taos their track lies east-west, but its optimal location is near water to symbolize a "lake of emergence." Today's runs occur in the piney hills near Stone Lake, 20 miles south of Dulce. Another indication of Pueblo origin are the aspen-and-cottonwood "kivas" which each team constructs at their end of the track; the running stretch itself stands for the section of the Milky Way where Sun and Moon had raced. For weeks ahead the boys train for the trials which determine the final line-up; their fervor exceeds that of the formal runs. Customarily runners were drawn from boys past

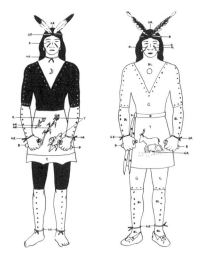

Jicarilla Apache relay racers, costume and body paint for Moon (l.) and Sun (r.) teams. G: gray. B: brown. GR: green. Y: yellow. R: red. BL: blue

Jicarilla Apache relay race

Jicarilla Apache relayers

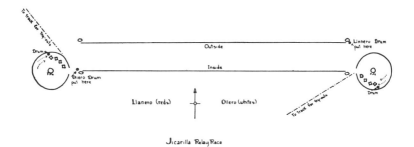

Jicarilla Apache relay track

puberty but not yet married. At one time all men were expected to participate at least once in their lives.

On their soles some rub ash from burned sunflowers to keep joints flexible. In shrines and on costumes custom dictates the placement of plumage from sandhill cranes, cliff swallows, black-necked stilts and a host of other fast-flyers. Warm-up dances circle to the pounding of pottery drums. Painted rocks indicate starting points on the track. Each side's colored banners crack in the wind. Intricate ground paintings are laid on the brush-kiva floors. Bodypaint and costuming evoke the mythic run they replicate: yucca headbands, shell earrings, feathers. Moon runners display cornstalks on their breechcloths and must go barefoot since buckskin has no place in the plant kingdom.

The actual racing is almost a come-down. The winning side enjoys little acclaim, tallies are not kept over the years. It is running as performance; it must be done. Today about 2,000 Jicarilla occupy a well-to-do 542,000-acre reservation about seventy-five miles west of Taos. In altered form, they still perform the mid-September relays. These Indians are successful cattlemen, and earn good incomes from leasing the product of ancient vegetation, oil. It can be said they still run to assure their survival from a dual economic base of plants and animals.

At one time southern California Indians also ran in accord with the movements of celestial bodies. After his death the Luiseño deity, Wuyoot, reappeared as the moon. Early Catholic padres grew used to seeing bonfires at the first sight of the new moon, followed by shouting, crashing of brush, and pounding of Indian feet. As Wuyoot had instructed the first people, thus they were to give their spirits to him; their running and shouting would let them enjoy long lives. At San Juan Capistrano Father Gerónimo Boscana learned further details of this new moon running and understandably stressed the resurrection motif.

The people distinguished New Moon running—called *hayic*—from ordinary foot races, known as *naamiq*. A line of twenty to fifty boys and men stripped down. Wood piles were lit as the first sliver of moon rose and the runners dashed barefoot into the night at a three-shout signal, everyone clucking in their throats to give the moon strength. At the close of his edition of Padre Boscana's journal, anthropologist John Peabody Harrington indulged in a paean to southern California Indian running and nudity:

"The custom (of going without clothes) is said to have made for lightness of foot, distance trotting, and all kinds of bodily process . . . the skin was so toughened that the feeling of flies on it was only pleasureable. . . . A sting or two from the California Harvesting Ant as one sprawled about on the ground was regarded as good medicine. . . . In writing about Indians it is sometimes refreshing for a moment to forget our rigid standpoint of superiority and to dream our way back into simple customs which underpopulation made possible, and to praise them.''

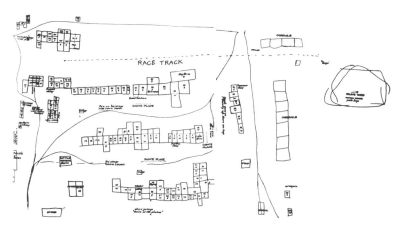

San Juan Pueblo, showing relay track

From the Indian village the trio of runners easily make the town of Taos in less than fifteen minutes, and sprint along plastered mud walls which seem to glow beneath the street lights. Dropping past the plaza their gait is constricted behind an oil truck, coughing exhaust with each gearing down. Thankfully they turn onto Rt. 3, the "old road" paralleling the Rio Grande Chiquito, and rise into the Sangre de Cristo Mountains where the air smells of dew and pine. Against the dark outline of an abandoned adobe the procession starts climbing a thousand feet up U.S. Hill to Picuris Pueblo some fifteen miles away.

A pattern emerges: a support van bearing fresh runners zooms ahead, covering precisely five miles before sidling over to the shoulder. Upcoming runners stretch and joke, sprawl across the road, piss, chat. Crawling up the incline appears the police car, red light revolving as it rides point. The boys yell encouragement to the little figures behind it, their legs pumping, a serpentine convoy on their tail. Something jars about their snail-like pace; it is an affront to the rule of the automobile. The cars behind the vulnerable figures of bone and flesh seem groaning to pull out and tear forward.

Fresh runners ready themselves. As the approaching boys grow larger, their paces seems faster, but more to the point, inexorable. The transfer of the pouch occurs with the speed of light, hand released to hand tightening. One is given the startling sense of having been left behind, as Wolf felt surprised by Terrapin.

From a metal-roofed farmhouse a Hispanic hard hat, coffee cup in hand, pauses before hauling himself into his four-wheel drive. It seems comparable to discovering a Japanese-American parade celebrating Pearl Harbor passing your front porch, but years dull history's sting. Hispanic bitterness that wasn't purged by the 1692 Reconquest has been redirected to the Anglo world which took away their land grants. Except for the T-shirts the Hopi boys are wearing the Indians haven't advertised the meaning of this event. Even if the man could see them up close, he probably wouldn't decipher the four white crosses against the black field on the quartered medallion emblazoned on the Hopi T-shirts: the four Spanish Catholic churches and priests destroyed by the Hopi.

Past Talpa the runners dip and climb around the road cut into the hillsides of Carson National Forest—the Camino Real which Don Diego de Vargas crossed in the 1690s during his Reconquest. Karl hopes for a juxtaposition of runners against Spanish adobes and we hustle ahead to Peñasco. Checking camera angles before a haggard old portal, we attract stares from farmers gassing up at the

Picuris runners passing pouch, 5 August 1980

hamlet's lone pump. One finally tells us we've been outfoxed, the runners have dropped into Picuris by a footpath.

We scurry there—"Mountain Gap" to its people—to find them come and gone. Picuris' annual fiesta is but five days away; when inhabitants scattered around the reservation's 15,000 acres will converge on San Lorenzo Church. As part of the traditional rain rites, the Northside folk ran against the Southside people in long distance races to a shrine atop sacred Jicarilla Mountain. I don't know if that tradition continues, but every San Lorenzo Day Picuris still holds relay races. Unlike at Taos, the strict team division is relaxed to make sure both sides are balanced with enough strong runners. In 1965 the Pueblo's race track was shortened by a new road, without significant objection.

Picuris today is shrunken from its former glory, when, at the end of the 16th century, it was among New Mexico's largest Pueblos. We finally locate three old timers behind the church who behave as if we were Spanish soldiers asking for the whereabouts of Luis Tupatu, Po'pay's Picuris lieutenant. One finally chin-motions toward the

Runner passing Black Mesa (near San Ildefonso) 5 August 1980

Rio Pueblo, where the Picuris boys have taken over from the Taos runners, and are advancing the pouch twenty-eight miles to San Juan Pueblo.

Further down Route 75 we find them being applauded by parents and friends. Decorated aprons over their running briefs simulate loin cloths. Hawks' bells jingle around their waists, and one older boy sports a bandoleer of clacking Yaqui shells. Their faces are streaked with paint, downy plumes dance on their crowns. Some have medicine pouches slung over their shoulders, containing, I'm told, cornmeal, flecked with turquoise.

Eddie All Runner, a seventeen-year-old, part-Cheyenne, part-Picuris lives with his mother in southern California. He flew out this week because, "They needed help. This only happens every 300 years, so I came for the Feast Day, and for this too. It's my way of being part of the Indian life, that's important to me no matter where I am." His father, Lionel, calls Eddie "my 1984 Olympic contender." In Del Rey Eddie runs with the Phidippides Club; for the past week, though, he has been making eight-mile laps before breakfast and at dusk in anticipation of today.

Interrupting our talk, Eddie crouches as cheering signals an upcoming runner. In slow motion he takes a few strides, arm stretched back. As the transfer is made doors slam, the leap-frogging continues to Dixon. Here the run's most unspoiled stretch detours southwest, below the Mesa de la Cejita. On this overland shortcut from Dixon to Velarde the runners bob and jump, rise and disappear over a roller-coaster succession of sagebrush and piñon hills. Struggling to keep up behind them three vehicles waffle up and down the sandy ruts like elephants.

Shortly before noon we come upon San Juan Governor Vincente Martinez, canes of office in hand, as he is hastening to the Pueblo's Southside small kiva. Martinez oversees one of the most fertile Pueblos, as nearly half of San Juan's 13,000 acres falls within a well-watered wedge between the Rio Chama and the Rio Grande. Just minutes after he positions himself before the kiva, runners trickle past the gathering audience. Cornmeal speckles their backs and hair as they are ushered into the dark room.

San Juan is the first and biggest of the six Tewa-speaking towns the runners will visit. Its race track runs 650 feet east to west on the north side, just behind the last row of connected house blocks. Traditionally San Juan's races pitted Summer people against Winter people—the town's two divisions. Its symbolism involved not only the sun, it also was a race for rain, as implied in its name, "rain-standing-falling." Alfonso Ortiz remembers when he was seven years old and began practising for the San Juan relays:

"I was at one end of the earth track which ran east to west like the path of the sun. The old man, who was blind and a wise elder among my people, called me to him and said, 'Young one, as you run, look to the mountain top,' and he pointed out the Tewa sacred mountain of the west, Tsikomo, Obsidian-Covered-Mountain. 'Keep your gaze fixed on that mountain,' the old man said, 'and you will feel the miles melt beneath your feet. Do this, and in time you will feel as if you can leap over bushes, trees, and even the river.' "

We learn the Hopis have suffered two setbacks. Before Picuris, Tom Kahe of Keam's Canyon skidded on gravel and is laid up with a sprained ankle. "Luckily we had our medicine woman," he said, prone in a van. "The EMT (emergency medical team) packed it in ice, but she cracked it back in place right there." More embarrassingly, after completing the obstacle course between Dixon and Velarde, the Hopis have gotten lost on the frontage road alongside Route 64—the principal Taos-to-Santa Fe highway.

It is practically 2:00 p.m. as disgruntled Hopis troop into the San Juan kiva. Inside they are surprised by a Hopi kachina priest, Preston Keevama from Second Mesa, who lives here now. He speaks in Hopi: "This isn't a fun run. It has a purpose. Carry this ear of blue corn, your mother, the entire way. As you go, she will give you strength. When you get back, plant from it, each of you. Now go your way, with strength and prayer." A new symbol and responsibility, the grey-blue ear of corn will stand for the Hopi's separate message to themselves.

Addressing the San Juan boys now bound for Nambe and San Ildefonso, Winter division elder John Trujillo prays in Tewa for the Great Spirit's blessing. This was how their grand-great-grandfathers banded together three centuries ago, he says. Now it is being done again. Treat each other as brothers, he says, and never give up your people's ways.

Outside the kiva tribal officials and police lean against sleek, radio-equipped cars and talk shop. Kids wheel about on bikes. Without fanfare a figure darts from the kiva entrance, heading for the old railroad road towards Santa Clara Pueblo.

Bruce Gomez entering Tesuque, 5 August, 1980

The event moves to the west bank of the Rio Grande.

Within an hour Santa Clara escorts pick up the pouch-carriers and all come in to watch the pueblo's official, Edwin Tafoya, receive the pouch from heavily breathing runners. Here the old foot-running track has a more southeasterly-northwesterly alignment, as it extends from the southern dance plaza and skirts the massive, free standing kiva to terminate not far from the Winter moiety house.

Now the Santa Clara boys are bound for San Ildefonso. We get there in good time ahead of them, and wait in the mothering shade of the great cottonwood which separates its plazas. Relay races are customarily held here on June 13, San Antonio Day; the track extends the full length of the southern plaza and, like Taos, breaks beyond the adobe perimeter. Cloud shade scuttles over the circular kiva, planted like a piece of memorial sculpture on the rise. Beneath the tree card tables holding Gatorade, apple juice and munchies await the runners. The San Ildefonso coach debates with his runners about the best route to Tesuque. Whoops from the north side signal the Santa Clarans; within five minutes the San Ildefonsons are trudging off.

The Hopis arrive in Tesuque first and wait for the others to catch up. The sun is high and hot. Dust rises along the alleys leading into this home village of the Tricentennial's runner-martyrs. Again the Hopi depart early, shortly followed by Tesuque boys and girls for the day's final stretch. While the Hopis stick to the highway, the locals take a more interesting route, nine miles on an unpaved lane which becomes Santa Fe's Tano Road. Auto traffic seems obsolete. The winding route overlooks a sea of piñon unbroken for miles as it lifts into the heights of the Sangre de Cristos.

Silence surrounds six-year-old Wenona Brascoupe as she gamely puffs towards Santa Fe, its hotels and condominiums just coming into sight. Three centuries ago it became the first and only white man's city to be conquered and occupied by North American Indians, by the ancestors of this girl holding the pouch in her small hand.

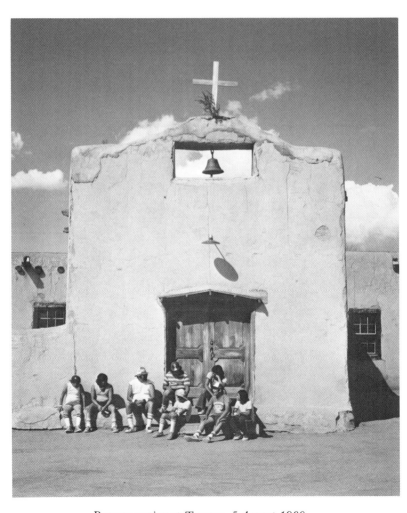

Runners resting at Tesuque, 5 August 1980

Runners between Zia and Jemez, 6 August 1980

3.

Santa Fe to Jemez
6 August

RECOVERY OF THE HOPI
KICK-STICK AT COCHITI
BLOODY RUNNER KACHINA OF SANTO DOMINGO
ZIA OPENS ITS ARMS
ORIGINS OF RITUAL RUNNING: AN ON-GOING DEBATE
RUNNERS' AIDS: TURTLE LEGS TO RABBIT HATS
RACE POTIONS AND TECHNIQUES AT JEMEZ
RUNNING AND HUNTING:
DEER, RABBITS AND THE OMAHA "BUFFALO RUNNERS"
RECEPTION AT JEMEZ

IT'S NOT HARD to understand why the Keresan-speaking villages the runners will reach today describe their cosmos as flat and angular. New Mexico's high country comes to a screeching halt at "The Descent," a black basaltic cliff which climaxes the Santa Fe plateau. In our rearview mirror New Mexico's capitol of Santa Fe rests like a sanctuary beneath the mountain wall.

The runners seem about to topple into the immensity of the lower Rio Grande Basin as we overtake them, one Hopi pounding the frontage road ahead of boys from San Juan, Tesuque, Santa Clara, and Taos. Looking south across swells of cholla and locoweed, the eye fixes on the low Cerrillos hills against the backdrop of the Ortiz Mountains, still further the 10,000-foot Sandias overlooking smog-bound Albuquerque, and off to the west, the grizzled Jemez peaks, thunderheads brooding over them.

Nineteen miles and two hours earlier nearly a hundred runners, their ranks swelled since yesterday, turned out of borrowed bunks in Santa Fe's Institute of American Indian Arts dorm. Leaving Santa Fe at sunrise, the starters picked their way along the broken curbs of Cerrillos Road, streaming traffic to their left, tacky food stands and greasy auto shops to their right. Hooking onto the frontage road they passed the oversize bleachers of Santa Fe's race track and at last breathed in open country. Another nineteen miles will bring them to Cochiti Pueblo which, unlike most pueblos reconstructed after the Revolt, still stands where Don Juan de Oñate found it nearly four centuries ago.

We hear the Hopis are still discontent over yesterday. There may be truth in the observation that Pueblo people avoid the spotlight, but that doesn't mean they like looking bad. Getting into San Juan an hour or so late was looking bad. Just as one must not stand too far out, one must not stand too far back. In the dorm last night they complained about fouled-up organization. From now on they run a tighter crew, their lapping this morning seems measured precisely at three-mile intervals.

From La Bajada they drop nearly 3,000 feet in about three miles, thigh muscles shuddering with each brake. At the base of the mesa the road to Cochiti and Santo Domingo is bumper to bumper with kids on car hoods, waiting for their own boys, ready to refresh them with styrofoam cups of water. The Hopi receive polite applause as they roll by first, like a delegation from another land.

The small village of Cochiti is bleaching out in the heat and blinding light. Three girl runners behind the Hopis breathe laboriously on the rise toward Pumpkin Kiva and stop at the hastily convened crowd hogging the shade beneath a two-story adobe. Once Cochiti's Easter festivities featured kick-stick races launched from this kiva. Along this road teams ran to markers beyond town, four races in all, each toward a different compass point to call in the rainclouds. Then everyone pitched in to clear the irrigation ditches of winter's debris.

John Bowannie tells me, "Our traditional races were for other things too, plenty of flour, chickens and food during the summer months." At age three Bowannie left the village, returning only a few years ago. In January he became governor. When the runner extends the pouch, Bowannie extracts its knotted cord and message as if they were artifacts. The town also seems caught off-guard by this running invasion. Bowannie does tell me, "This race brings to the attention of the public that in 1680 the Pueblos pulled all their strength together to resist the dominant society. Today it seems they still don't want to recognize us as having unique, sovereign powers—as the United States recognizes other nations."

I am aware that Cochiti is famed for its old-style log drums, and that ceremonial life persists. But I know that it permitted 4,000 acres to be inundated for a recreational lake for tourists, and I have read that Easter Sunday races had not been held for years and runner-kachinas have not appeared since 1945. This progressive community is what I see reflected in Governor Bowannie's sunglasses. I am curious about what we will find next at Santo Domingo, reputedly the most conservative Pueblo of all.

Lightning glitters in the dark Jemez skies as we glide through head-high cornfields and irrigation ditches. Flooding has been known to endanger this 74,000-acre reservation, nearly four times the size of Cochiti. We enter by way of the northernmost of its nine parallel avenues, and pull up by the cottonwoods lining the large ditch which winds before St. Dominic's, its balconied facade painted with cavorting horses. Santo Domingo strikes me as justifying the title, "city-state."

I'm not surprised when Karl manages only one shot from a handcrank Hasselblad before an elder, grey hair elegantly knotted behind his neck, motions for him to know better. No sooner do the runners arrive than they are surrounded and sequestered in the community center. Santo Domingans are masters at letting you know when they've got private business to take care of.

Customarily their races take place on feast days: San Juan (June 25), San Pedro (June 29), Santiago (July 26), San Lorenzo (August 10). Despite their fortunate location, they run "to help the clouds come out and for rain." This region counts on July and August downpours for a third of its rainfall, when dry gulleys become brown rapids. The runners are dedicated both to helping fire-sun stay on his way and drawing water-clouds to the crops.

On the field south of St. Dominic's, author Vincent Scully saw a footrace a dozen years ago, but his account is meager; the Pueblo has never made it easy for investigators to study their traditions. When he visited in the 1920s, photographer Edward S. Curtis was told about a variety of rain-bringing spirits—kachinas—who challenged men at "overtaking" races. If the kachina lost, he yielded up rain, clouds and game. A play of human-and-spirit interaction, Curtis' account has the younger men ready for the dare, but their elders pretend to restrain them lest they lose and the fields dry up. In disgust one runner-kachina threatens to withhold his gifts and begins running off, the eagle feathers on his arms lifting like wings. The youths break out and manage to catch him ten miles later. It seems a lesson to the young to take kachinas seriously, even though, after their initiation into the kachina cult they know them to be impersonated by their relatives.

Once this runner-kachina helped a Santo Domingan enact a bloody revenge. Hunting near a holy spring, a boy from the Pueblo was ambushed by a hunter from Zia Pueblo. The dead lad's brother donned one of the runner-kachina masks, sneaked into the Zia plaza, and challenged the murderer to a race. As they circled the mesa east of Zia the kachina played with his victim, catching him, then circling and taunting him before falling behind. Away from view, however, he sliced off his head with a flint knife.

Probably the real episode followed white contact, since its chase sequence ends with the runner-kachina on horseback, galloping for home pursued by mounted Zians. He leaps from a bluff to the river and hides overnight in a cave, arriving home safely holding his trophy by its hair. A new kachina was thus created. At Cochiti, however, where a version of the tale is told, the mask of this Bloody Hand kachina was eventually destroyed because of the malignant power associated with it. At Santo Domingo, there is no apparent disapproval for the desecration of kachina attire; when this runner kachina is impersonated today, his gear includes the bloody "thunder knife," ornamented with dangling strands of hair.

The runners have left surreptitiously from Santo Domingo and we quietly leave without photos through its long streets, feeling closed out by the disinterested glances of passers-by. "Stern, strict and grand," wrote Vincent Scully. "The stiffest-necked of all the Pueblos," said Charles Lummis. "Stubborn and indomitable," felt Frank Waters. Its horizontal authority seems a counterpoint to the vertical impact of Taos to the north. "Complicated and remote" Taos, was Scully's impression. There you stand on the hand-hewn Ponderosa logs which make up the ancient bridge and feel your curiosity as embarrassingly exposed as you do here. Around you adobe blocks ascend lopsidedly skyward. As the mountain backdrop magnifies their force the miniature town becomes monumental before your eyes. Taos and Santo Domingo, like Acoma and Walpi

Runners heading for Jemez, 6 August 1980

to the west—almost islands, unreachable, beyond description.

Backtracking ten miles to Bob's Grocery in Peña Blanca, we munch sandwiches and down Dr. Peppers in the shade with two French journalists. Trendy but genial, they have stumbled upon the run unprepared and are beside themselves. Meanwhile the runners have no such respite—until a short break at Santa Ana Pueblo. We miss their entry into San Felipe's classical plaza. They then turn off from the Santa Fe-to-Albuquerque highway and follow Route 44 along the Jemez River, hitting the Pueblos which are like stepping stones back into the northern New Mexico wilderness.

Commanding a shallow mesa the ramparts of Zia Pueblo look like an Ethiopian citadel from medieval times. None of its 16,669 acres tie it into the Rio Grande and its water is brackish from a salt source four miles north. Zia's survival has always been precarious; it is reputed to be an impoverished, outcast community. Yet neighbors and tourists alike covet its pottery, decorated with the famous bird and sun designs.

The Zia people stand sentinel-like on their stone terraces. A kiva roof is crowded with onlookers. Across a wooden bridge the caravan of runners, cars and pickups weave into view. In the distance is Roadrunner Mountain, site of Zia's ritual runs around its base. The birds are numerous there, and runners seek their power as they race for the sun and rain.

Passing a maze of livestock corrals, the runners lift up the road curving around the mesa. We hurry through the zig-zag alleys, emerging into the narrow plaza. A potency about the open area makes me retreat into a doorway. The plaza is a tableau: as if on stage, two lines of women stand with traditional pots and gourd ladles at their feet. Only the dome of blue sky seems privy to this domain. At my side is an immobile woman in clay-streaked smock, her hands crackling with drying potter's slip. She stares at a group of older men stationed around a large, tipping white cross. Fresh sand has been strewn and raked, the furrows swirling around two rocks jutting up like icebergs which dominate the open space. One is the home of Mountain Lion and protects Zia's animals and keeps away disease. The other is the home of Twin War Gods and protects Zia from witches. (I wonder if the story is true that during the Revolt the Zia people drove their priest through the village tied to the back of a pig, then rode him themselves before killing him.) No one has made a sound.

Single file the runners spill into the plaza. The quiet cracks with trills of praise. The women bend to their jars and hurl arcs of water over the runners passing through their aisle. The spray gleams like an arbor of light. One by one they collide into the huddle beside the cross. Prayers are chanted and cornmeal daubed on soaking backs and hair. A Zia holy man presents the Hopis with a fluffy eagle plume. Some of the boys are openly weeping. One blurts out a thanksgiving prayer in English: "Make your life and grow old."

Although the leg to Jemez beckons—four miles on a backroad, shortcutting the Hispanic town of San Ysidro—the bunching around the cross seems unwilling to come apart. Women sprinkle the leftover water in their jars on Mountain Lion and War Gods rocks. Together the Hopis repeat the refrain which now booms over the plaza: "Make your life and grow old."

Choctaw Stick Game Runner, 1834

Running traditions in Pueblos like Zia, Jemez and Isleta raise questions about the roots of Indian athleticism. Do they lie in mythology and ritual, or is that an overlay on *a priori* reasons for organized running: communication, warfare, hunting? This is often a dividing line for students of culture. Hard-headed anthropologists search for practical determinants to the origin of cultural complexes like ceremonial running; others maintain that man has always sought to influence his fate through symbolic action. While the pragmatic scholars have generally been an older breed, this is not the case in the minimal examination paid to Indian sports. In his 1933 diary of Hopi life at Old Oraibi, the ethnographer Mischa Titiev mused, "When interpreting racing don't overlook the practical importance of running in ancient times before horses and burros were known. War, too, formerly demanded fleetness of foot. Realistic factors probably underlay the original stress on running and were later rationalized into the current belief that racing is for mimetic magic for quickly bringing rain and crops."

But an earlier researcher had arrived at a different conclusion. Crowning a lifelong study of primitive games, Steward Culin, world-traveller and trained Sinologist, wrote *Games of the North American Indians,* published in 1905 soon after he became curator of the Brooklyn Museum. Culin exhausted the ethnographic literature, and did field work in the Southwest. He separated Indian games into those of chance and dexterity. He believed that both secular and religious games had their taproot in the "ancient compulsion" toward symbolic enactment for the purpose of "sympathetic magic." They were played and performed to drive away sickness, produce rain, fertilize crops. They were the instruments of rites or had descended from ceremonial observances. In the countless games he had studied Culin found nuances and reflections of the origin myths which gave tribespeople their identity.

Less interested in resolving outsiders' explanations than perpetuating the running itself, Indians, when pressed, have buttressed both points of view. Suggesting the practical motivation, a Hopi of the Horn clan said, "Long ago when the Hopi had no sheep, no horses, no burros, they had to depend for game-capturing on their legs. They then had to cultivate their legs, think much and pray much to make them swift. Men strove in earnest to rival each other in fast running, that is why the races were run . . ." Yet another Hopi, from the Goat kiva, explained: "It has always been well for the Hopi to be able to run swift and far, and in these races the Cloud spirits rejoice to see the youth run, and he who is fastest wins. His prayers for rain will have special virtue." Finally, the Hopi preach

Hopi Rabbit Hunter, 1924

its general contribution to health; running lifts the heart, dispels sadness, firms up the flesh and renews one's vigor.

Indian runners relied on powers beyond their own abilities to help them run for war, hunting, and sport. To dodge, maintain long distances, spurt for shorter ones, to breathe correctly and transcend oneself called for a relationship with strengths and skills which were the property of animals, trails, stars and elements. Without their tutelage and beneficence one's potential could never be realized. Runners often seemed suspended between the source of their power and its fulfillment in purposeful action. The most frequent source was animals and their use of animal modes of motion took intriguing form.

To the Chemehuevi of California the Mountain Sheep might confer their agility, giving a lame man the ability to run up a sheer cliff. When the Hidatsa woman, Buffalo Bird Woman, was a girl along the upper Missouri River, she delighted in wearing her father's hunting cap, a helmet of buffalo hide with two ears stuffed with antelope hair to suggest jackrabbit ears. His dream of rabbits had led him to believe this talisman would give him their gift of darting and dodging. Tribes might possess contradictory estimations of such creatures. In the Southeast, Cherokee stickball runners stayed clear of rabbits, believing the animals lost their wits and scared easily. Nor would the Cherokee runner eat frogs' legs; instead they rubbed their calves with greasy turtle legs to gain the turtles' strength and purity.

These ballplayers sought animal and plant powers before each game. Birds-of-prey feathers in their hair (preferably eagle) lent keenness of sight. Deer tails offered speed. Body paint concocted from the burned patch where a honey-locust tree had been struck by lightning tightened their flesh. Muscles were toughened by a bath in catgut root. They prayed to the Red Bat to help them dodge, to the Red Deer for speed, to the Red Hawk for sharp vision, and to the Red Rattlesnake that their voices might terrify their adversaries. They made themselves composites of their flora and fauna.

Names could help stabilize one's running talents. One Apache was called He Moves Lightly And Quickly. All his life the Sioux warrior, Running Holy, had his prowess paired with his spiritual leanings. Among the Hupa of northern California the name Runs Down From The Hill was possibly given to someone skilled at a form of "power running" found among the nearby Yurok. The Hunkpapa Sioux artist, Running Antelope, earned his name after he spent five hours running down an adult antelope and killing it with his hands.

A boy growing up in Jemez Pueblo, where running is prominent in ritual life, learned early to seek animal assistance. Jemez' important running event is the autumn harvest races on the second week of September; if there is no frost, they are also held the end of October. When the river ice broke up, Jemez boys scoured the mountains for wild plants to brew as emetics. Supervised by the tribe's Fire Society, their training period opened with a four-day retreat: singing, hard fasting and prayer. Joe Sando, a Jemez writer, explains that "youngsters were building up strength and at the same time collecting the natural foods of rabbits. With various other plants, this mixture served as our 'vitamins,' so we could become fast as rabbits. At the same time it purified our system."

Older boys combed the forests for pine, fir and scrub oak boughs which deer eat, adding heart of Spanish Dagger. This "tea bag" was tied with split yucca and allowed to steep. Meanwhile the runners buried prayer feathers around their practise areas to appease the land's spirits and so avoid stubbed toes. Before the intense five-to-ten mile training runs every day, runners drank and vomited up these brews. Afterwards the dessicated plants were laid at the runners' shrine on East Mesa.

Runners were also aided by the elements. "For the tree, the wind is a reminder to get exercise," Pueblo children might hear from their grandmother. "We like to run out toward the hills," a Pueblo girl told psychologist Robert Coles, "and sit down near the grass and the bushes; the wind excites them; they sing, and so do we. My mother laughs and she sings, too; she calls one song her wind song. She made us learn the words a long time ago: 'Come and be strong/We can be strong/We welcome you/We miss you/We will wait for you to return!' " Further north, on the Plains, an Arapaho Ghost Dancer also sang to the wind, "Our father, the Whirlwind, by

Isleta foot races, 1896

its aid I am running swiftly.''

Running in warfare often had its supernatural cast. Among the Hopi, the best runners were dispatched into Navajo country to search the enemy's hogans for hair combings, saliva and food. Back home this would be buried as ''bait''; a fire laid atop them would weaken the Navajo before a forthcoming fight. At Isleta Pueblo, where racing and war, according to Elsie Clews Parsons ''are conceptually and ceremonially related,'' what survived of that connection was the scalp ritual racing. The traditional enemies are again the Navajo; the Isleta kiva becomes a trophy house for safeguarding their ''scalps.'' Care is taken to purify the runners, as though they were warriors returning from battle. Perhaps this running rite is a trace memory of the war party necessary to acquire those scalps. Elders used far-seeing crystals to divine whether high winds, hail, or tacks in the street might endanger their men. They also foretold which runners would have their queue, or *chongo*, yanked in the relay race, and by ''curing'' their runners made sure the opposition could

not induce cramps. When these war-related races were held every three or four years, Isletans ran with arrowpoints in their mouths for speed.

Running was just as vital to the quest for food. The Yuki knew that deer instinctively travelled in a wide circle; relayers posted along their path could drive the animals to exhaustion. Pueblo hunters also knew that steady tracking would wear the deer down since it was their nature to graze frequently; kept on the move they soon tired. Navajos requiring unpunctured deer skins for ritual mats would also run down deer, then smother them with corn pollen. Today this is rarely practised and road kills supply Navajo singers with unblemished hides.

On deer hunts some Pueblo runners carried an agate fetish in-laid with turquoise, shaped like a mountain lion and blessed by a priest. The cat's prowess kept deer anxious and moving. Again, if meat was for a ritual, the kill should be bloodless, the animal thrown and smothered. Pre-hunt rituals bound hunters in a symbiotic relationship with their game, whose distinctive traits were almost as desired as their meat. In a way, their teachers became their prey.

Pueblo running after rabbits was highly ritualized. Because of their spunk, the Hopi prized black-tailed jackrabbits over cottontails. In winter their hunters descended the mesas before sunrise, searching for tracks in the snow. Good hunters brought back three or four by noon. Better known are the Pueblo communal hunts, ceremonial vestiges of a time when their ancestors had to hunt collectively or starve.

In the mid-1890s a white farmer assigned to Jemez joined a rabbit drive. The "war captain" placed his beaters wielding old-fashioned clubs around a square mile of wooded ridge which bottlenecked into a tight ravine. A deer and coyote were flushed into the pile of frantic rabbits. Furious bludgeoning ensued. In Jemez' town square, the carcasses were laid end to end, heads directed to the setting sun. As the hunters filed past, they stroked the animals' fur, dribbled cornmeal on them, and prayed to inherit their agility.

When Isleta held its annual hunt, the lead beater brought a stone wolf fetish so as to be guided by the rabbit's natural enemy. For Pueblos who believed that the soul is breath, the dying animal's muzzle might be lifted to the hunter's mouth so he could inhale that soul. At Hopi, where rabbits are classified as a crop along with the harvest of corn and squash, an impersonator of the powerful spirit, Masau, wears a rabbit's mask soaked in blood when he oversees the autumn yield. He chases pickers about the fields with a cotton-padded club. "All this running about is good for the crops," they say, the rabbit's spriteliness offering a healthy model for general life and growth.

In the Great Basin these communal drives corralled antelope. Surrounded on the desert, the animals were chased on foot into V-shaped corrals or long fiber nets, where they were killed by clubs or arrows. Such methods go back centuries; in White Dog Cave Ruin in northeastern Arizona archeologists found a net woven from nearly five miles of spun hair and milkweed fiber which was probably strung across narrow canyons for mass hunts. The Hopi consider

I'shibazhi, Omaha Buffalo Runner

deer and antelope relatives because both double back and shoot out
at right angles on the chase. During the Hopi's Snake-Antelope
Festival, the participants are goaded to run like antelopes in a ritual
race underlain with both fertility and war motifs.

Scouting for animals was another runner's duty. Novices
learned to sense and behave like the animals they pursued. "We use
boys for scouting," Cochiti governor Jose Trujillo told Edith Wilson forty years ago. "The way white men use dogs. The boys we take
to teach them the habits of the animals. We make little dogs of them,
making them run and scent and listen noiselessly like a lizard freezes
itself into one position. And they have to learn to balance themselves
so that they don't break a twig and frighten away an animal."

After the buffalo-hunting Omaha of the central plains acquired
horses they retained "buffalo runners," called *wado'be,* meaning
"those who look." From a man named I'shibazhi, who ran for his
people during their final hunt, Omaha writer Francis La Flesche
heard how the hunt leader, known as the *watho,* would command
some twenty seasoned runners: "Come and secure knowledge of the
land for me."

They canvassed the countryside, scanning the sky for crows,

singing to them, for crows were their scouts to buffalo. Pinpointing the herd's location, they ran home. Instead of charging in with the news, they signalled from a hilltop by a pantomime known as the *waba'ha*—one man running from right to left, a second from a left to right, criss-crossing each other. The Sacred Pole and White Buffalo Hide were carried to a greeting spot by the Seven Chiefs; the hide hung over a frame to resemble a reclining buffalo. In a low voice the first runner described the herd's size and location. When a second man verified his report, camp was struck. If the animals were nearby boys began rounding up buffalo ponies for a coordinated attack.

By the time whites took note of Indian running, these magical aids and mystical purposes permeated native warfare and hunting as well as athletics. Fasting, sexual abstinence, emetics, and dietary rules prepared men and women for the practical and spiritual rewards of the running experience, goals which were probably inseparable from the beginning.

Runners reception at Jemez, 6 August 1980 (photograph by Sam Bingham).

We've jack-knifed twelve miles north from Zia, into the volcanic highlands on the Jemez River's eastern bank to this Towa-speaking outpost. The "people of the canyon" gave the Spanish fits before, during and after the 1680 Rebellion. Near the southeast corner of the Jemez plaza, in front of the lead priest's house, I notice a clump of rotting rabbit skins wired to an electrical pole—the ceremonial hunt must have been held recently.

To the west, eroding mesa planes topple southwards behind level table buttes, while Parajito Peak falls in from the east like a tidal wave. The canyon wall behind me has long yielded obsidian for the ancestors of these people, who once occupied a number of villages to the north. As usual, the Hopis show first. Jemez officials sprint alongside with instructions about cutting across the plaza—through a cooling shower as at Zia—to make a courtesy call at the *cacique's* doorway before circling into the North Plaza beyond our view.

I'm reminded of a Jemez memory N. Scott Momaday once shared with me. The resident schoolteacher's kid, Scott was usually on the outside of Pueblo rituals looking in. One night he awoke to the sound of shuffling feet moving urgently near his window. He parted the curtains in time to see a night patrol of *caciques,* the village's ruling priesthood, running witches out of the village.

The Hopis are joined by the Jemez runners who took over halfway from Zia. They tromp in a body into the main plaza. All eyes are riveted on a 76-year-old man in front wearing face paint, eagle plume, decorated breechcloth, and blue canvas deck shoes. He is Lucas Toledo, of whom people tell you fondly, "that old man, he's always running." Ten years ago he entered and won the race up Pike's Peak (14,110 feet) in the 65 and over category. The solemn phalanx he leads this afternoon seems to honor the high place of running here, along with commemorating those messengers who gave Jemez the signal in 1680 to kill Father Juan de Jesus and bury him beside their kiva.

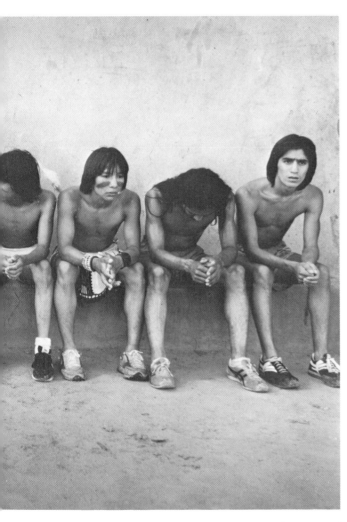

Runners resting beneath Jemez kiva, 6 August 1980

Acoma kick-stick racers, c. 1905

4.

Laguna to Acoma
7 August

COMPETITIVE RACES: ARCTIC TO HIGH PLAINS
EPIC OF PART-SKY-WOMAN, THE CHIPPEWA AMAZON
RACING INTO OLD AGE, LITTLE WOLF'S VICTORY
LONG DISTANCE AT JEMEZ
RUNNING FOR THE SUN'S STRENGTH:
ISLETANS ON THE "SUN ROAD"
A BRAZILIAN INDIAN NATIONAL SPORT: "LOG RUNNING"
THE MESSAGE REACHES ACOMA

TUCKED IN A RUGGED PASS, Laguna's shoebox houses and tangled utility poles pile up the steep knoll as if seeking protection from St. Joseph of the Lake church. We cross San Jose bridge and climb to the apparently deserted summit. I've turned up little on Laguna running. Its mythology does describe the earliest Lagunans emerging out of the underworld in the midst of a kick-stick race. A year after the first Protestant missionary settled here in 1851, the Pueblo was visited by ethnographer Henry Schoolcraft, who wrote that New Year's Day: "When the governor requires anything done, he sends one or two old fellows who act as town criers, and shout out their message at the foot of each ladder. These Indians are capital runners. They travel with ease forty or fifty miles between sun and sun"—roughly the distance the relayers are supposed to be covering this morning from Isleta. Today the Hopis are laying over in Jemez.

But the runners haven't shown yet. Our footfalls echo against the closed wooden doorways and plaster walls. Entering the gleaming white church, I marvel at the vegetal fecundity of the freehand Indian-painted mural which wraps the interior, its hills and corn so bold against the formal crucifixion altarpiece. Outside we find the plaza hidden behind a screen of houses, its molded bancos suggestive of prehistoric yards and ballcourts. Laguna and Acoma ancestors are supposed to hail from the cliff-dwellers of Mesa Verde. This sculpted space on top of the hill seems a last heirloom from that heritage.

Downslope two cars scoot to the highway with exaggerated importance. We scramble for our pickup, disappointed the little plaza won't be the setting for the reception. Instead the runners are met perfunctorily at a turnout below town. Perhaps it is appropriate; Laguna did not even exist before the Pueblo Revolt. In 1880 its conservative faction angrily departed for Mesita and Isleta, leaving behind a community somewhat ambivalent over its traditional identity. Most of the over 5,400 people who call the 420,000-acre reservation home are proud to belong to New Mexico's most acculturated Pueblo. Here I sense a subtle dislocation between the nostalgia of the Tricentennial participants for a more nationalistic yesteryear and the everyday worries of their parents' generation who must make these Pueblos function in modern times. Their visit might also be awkward because Pueblos rarely conduct rituals without rehearsal; this non-Indian genre of historical symbolism continues to take everyone by surprise.

At the highway I ask a carload of Laguna runners in blue warm-up suits for directions. Emmett Hunt Jr., a long distance champion at New Mexico State University, is at the wheel. His father, the local high school coach, was recently featured in *Sports Illustrated*'s "Running to Nowhere," an article which raised hackles here six months back because it speculated on the anxieties Pueblo athletes felt about competition, and emphasized their failures rather than successes. No matter what truth might have been in the piece, many Indians responded as if it was both an insult and an invasion of privacy.

They're turning south at the Acomita junction, Hunt says, then making a cross-country haul to the Pueblo. We pick up the caravan's tail toward "Sky City," constructed on a seventy-acre sandstone monolith which Captain Hernando de Alvarado called in 1540 "the strongest position ever seen in the world."

Chippewa runner's ankle weight

While stressing ritual running and mystical participation it should be underscored that Indians everywhere relished rough and ready competition. Because our sportsview is spectator dominated, we tend to pay as much attention to the postmortems of a sports event as we do when the experience is happening in its time and place. Who wins, how ratings are shuffled and where stars proceed from here preoccupy us. Public games are steps toward money and fame climbed by celebrities whose achievements we savor through the electronic aftertaste of slow-motion replay.

Non-Indians might minimize the rabid allegiance of fans during traditional Indian races, since once the finish line is crossed it often seems as if the event had never happened. Observers are surprised when the Tarahumara who wins a two-day race for his team walks away virtually ignored. There is a sense of anticlimax as the victor assumes normal stature and life goes on. If the race has pitted village halves against each other, neither schemes to reverse things next year. When they come together to run relays against each other it is the *together* that becomes crucial, not the *against*. Bewitching, power-building and exorcising might precede the race, and during the excitement a here-and-now favoritism could reach fever pitch. But, afterwards, something else takes center stage. An instant replay would mean you weren't all there when the real thing was going on.

Another difficulty in translating Indian sports to white fans is the lessened emphasis on professional heroes. Tribal society is private, and generally regulates the signal moments of its members' lives. Being a star amounts to a run-on peak experience, inappropriate in the Pueblo view. It tends to usurp others of their moments in the sun—puberty, marriage, old age—or even moderate acclaim for special talents. Moreover, Indian fans did not usually project fantasies of athletic success onto public figures, since nearly everyone ran. These generalities have their exceptions, as will be seen among the Chippewa and Maricopa, but similar undercurrents and meanings have kept white observers from grasping the tenor, protocol and purpose of native sports events.

The formats for races varied widely. In the Montana high country the Crow used a 300-yard track, and had a hard time controlling jump-starters. Most races began a dozen times before they got underway. To the east, in present-day North Dakota, the Mandan cleared a three-mile track, formed like a giant horseshoe, so that start and finish lines were but a hundred yards apart. Camp criers announced the race days ahead. Betting in blankets, buffalo robes, quilled shirts and leggings took a while because backers had to equalize their stakes. At the appointed time onlookers thronged within the curved track. Pairs of barefoot, painted runners would be dispatched until the track was packed. Three heats were necessary before winners might receive their red-painted feathers, victory tokens to be exchanged for spoils. Then all plunged into the cool Missouri.

In the land of the Osage along the present-day Kansas/Oklahoma border, an early nineteenth century chief named Black Dog constructed a race track to keep his warriors in trim. A length of two and half miles, it ran north-south in today's Rogers County, Oklahoma. Black Dog invited neighboring tribes to challenge his men. It was valuable training for the days when Osage couriers ran back and forth on the Black Dog Trail for the Confederacy. Inter-tribal running contests were also held in upper New York State between the Iroquoian tribes and the Missisauga of Ontario.

Far to the north the Nunivak Eskimo held short foot races during their Bladder Feast, a fourteen-day ritual held during "worst of the

Eskimo racers

moon"—January. The running honors the dead, whose spirits accompany the runners. In recent times Alaskan Eskimo Fourth of July festivities have included races. As a boy in the village of Gambell on St. Lawrence Island, Nathan Kalkianak was reluctant to join his village's celebration. "I didn't want to be in the race while there were so many people watching . . . I didn't care a bit about winning," he says in the autobiography taken down by Charles Hughes. Nevertheless, he won, and yet, "Oh I felt more bashful now . . . I seemed to talk to my parents in a funny way . . . the old folks were pestering me with praises and congratulations which I didn't like very much." That afternoon Kalkianak watched an "old fashioned" Eskimo race between grownups. Runners started from the village and ran along the north shore up to the mountain, then circled its base to Lake Troutman, returning via the shoreline. Anyone who stuck the whole way was considered a substantial runner.

Contrasting with Kalkianak's inhibition about prominence is the tale of the Chippewa amazon, Part-Sky-Woman. According to anthropologist Ruth Landes, native women of the Great Lakes enjoyed full athletic acceptance. Like men, Landes writes, women runners received "the negative face of acclaim. Defeated rivals, generally women, may knife them, sicken them with 'bad medicine,' and sometimes fall in abject fear before them. The successful woman develops a complementary attitude, a sneering sadism. She cannot carry this attitude far in any other relationship, but in this one sphere her behaviour precisely duplicates that allowed to successful men in all relationships."

Part-Sky-Woman's career was launched when her "spontaneous vision" of a cloud bestowed its lightness, speed and strength upon her. That spring the Hudson Bay Trading Co. Post at Fort Francis sponsored races and offered ribbons, shawls and silks as prizes for the mile—a half-mile out and back. After a private session with her cloud, Part-Sky-Woman ran off with the three top awards.

For eight years she repeated the feat. Jealous rivals tried unsuccessfully to wheedle her secret from her. When she failed to appear the tenth year, a Chippewa woman from the United States named Bird Woman took the honors. But the next year Part-Sky-Woman staged a comeback. Before the race she smudged her moccasins to protect her legs from evil. As she and Bird Woman were running neck and neck "Part-Sky-Woman could hear that Bird Woman was out of breath, and the woman said, 'I guess you will beat me,' and Part-Sky-Woman answered, 'I don't know. I do not care to win this race!'" Once the woman had sprinted ahead of her, Part-Sky-Woman addressed the shadow of her guardian cloud, "Now is the time to help me out, you that told me I would have fun. It would be shameful if I got beat." Right away she felt her body light as a feather, and, as if she were running on air, she passed the woman.

We don't know if Part-Sky-Woman employed any earthly aids to gain strength, but one Chippewa technique has been recorded to make runners feel "light-footed." Around their ankles they tied thin bags filled with lead shot. In 1888 a champion runner walked twenty-three miles after dinner wearing these weights, and the next morning won a foot race of a hundred yards in ten and a quarter seconds.

The story continues as one of Part-Sky-Woman's frustrated opponents slashes her face with a crooked knife. But the champion will not be cowed. The Hudson's Bay trader promotes her in races held in the white town of Kenora; she handily whips a featured white woman, a white man, and the trader rakes in a profit. There she is spotted by a young Indian who marries her. For four years she again abandons the field. Then her old wound becomes infected, as if her rivals are still bent upon revenge. Part-Sky-Woman appears to take this as a challenge, and, the story goes, returns to running and field hockey and never loses. She proclaims: "It's alright if I have to talk through my nose because of what the old Indians did to me. Only if they break my legs will I not be able to run anymore." But no one will compete against her now for she had proven herself to be a *manido*, a superhuman spirit.

Whenever the Chiricahua Apache planned a lengthy stay at a campsite they would pace off a footracing track about two hundred "steps" long. When the race was underway, old men kept time by counting for their runners; one Apache remembered a runner making the distance by the count of eleven. The starters did not crouch but braced themselves, and were launched by a "One, Two, Go" signal. Among both the Chiricahua and Mescalero Apache of the Southwest, women raced men for short distances. Visiting the Mescalero in the 1860s, Major John C. Cremony observed the mile, 100-yard, and 300-yard races; he was struck by a lovely seventeen-year-old who easily outran all her male competitors in the half-mile.

Indians also enjoyed specialty races. Along the Northwest Coast canoeing generally replaced running as the popular contest. But the Kwakiutl invented—besides regular running and walking races—one-legged hopping heats as well as forward and backward somersault races, from one end of their seaside villages to the other.

Old age was rarely a barrier to running. Tarahumaras and Hopis still run well beyond their sixties. The Navajo held an "old man's race," along with regular eight-mile races and girls' races. Unlike the white man's "on your mark, get set, go," they began their runs with a 1-2-3-4 count. As in a folktale brought to life, old-timers sometimes demonstrated how experience could outdo un-tutored vigor. The Cheyenne Wooden Leg liked to tell how Chief Little Wolf, a famous long-distance man in his youth, whipped the Sioux. The Oglala Sioux and the Cheyenne were moving camp together, and a Cheyenne goaded, "It appears that the Cheyennes

Navajo "Old Man's Race"

must go a little more slowly in order not to run away from their friends the Sioux." There was some more of this back and forth until a Sioux challenged Little Wolf to a foot race. Tipis were pitched and everyone came out for the fun.

Little Wolf was well over fifty; the Sioux was in his prime. Blankets and other goods were wagered; a three-to-four mile track was measured. At the crack of a pistol, both dashed towards the tipis. Up to the last mile, remembered Wooden Leg, the young man held first place, but he was at full throttle. When he started to falter, Little Wolf inched up and came in a good hundred yards ahead.

Because so much Pueblo racing is embedded in rites from which outsiders are excluded, first-hand accounts, outside of the Taos relays, are not common. During her work at Jemez Pueblo Elsie Clews Parsons awoke one September morning to glimpse the flowing hair and rippling breechcloths of the harvest racers arriving from

Red Rock, but most of her Jemez material remains second-hand. In the 1930s, however, an Albuquerque writer named Clee Woods, close to some Jemez families, was allowed a more relaxed look at the harvest runs.

At Jemez nearly every season featured its running event. In spring, before the irrigation ditches were opened, kick-stick races were held—as at Cochiti. Over spring and summer there were hardy retreats and training sessions in the mountains. At the same time relay races were staged along North Street. In winter, the runner kachina, Black Paint All Over, arrived to challenge able-bodied men and give them good luck in hunting. Rigorous training anticipated the five-to-six mile races of September and October.

They began outside the village, where runners collected before sunrise. Joe Sando writes, "A selected person would stand about fifty yards in front of a row of runners holding a trophy, a green corn-stalk. Directing the stalk in the four directions, he prayed to each, ending with the south. Prayer sticks tied to the stalk gave it power, made it a trophy.

"He cried out four times, finally pointing east, and everyone broke after the man with the cornstalk. The fastest man earns his day of glory by overtaking the man with this trophy. But he may only carry it a few yards before another overtakes him. Thus you have dashmen followed by those who may be good at different distances, as in our American races—220, 880, mile, and so forth—until by the time the runners are reaching the village, the long distance experts are closing in.

"As in any race one has to use strategy to accomplish whatever you plan. The man in best condition for longer distances is generally the one who finally takes the trophy to his home. The cornstalk is five to six feet long and awkward to handle while trying to speed. One learns to switch from right to left hand in carrying it. For the shorter distances, usually the same day, an ear of corn wrapped with fir branches is used. It's easier to carry, like a relay baton."

Although these ritual runs were dedicated toward a robust harvest, when Clee Woods relived them it was purely as a sports event:

Just as the sun rounded up over a wide *mesa* the runners tensed. The four starters watched. Then one of them let out a sudden sharp cry and all four of them broke up the road. Behind them the twenty-five runners leaped to the race like flushed quail.

In a moment a seventeen-year-old lad was in the lead. Rapidly he closed the distance between him and the starter who still carried the bundle of cornstalks. Soon he was passing the starter and this man handed him the bundle.

A second runner forged up behind the leader with the corn-stalk bundle. They fought it out there for nearly a quarter of a mile, this seventeen-year-old and his older challenger. The challenger had the best of it and the seventeen-year-old passed the bundle to him. That is the inviolate rule . . . little fellows of course played out fast. But it was good training for them, building up in them the spirit of the race and its traditions for the day when they'd be young men and real contenders in the pack.

It was the young fellows who'd been to Indian schools who were the foxy ones. Six or eight of them were lying back just behind the leader. They were content to let him set the pace—and be handicapped with that bundle! Let him wear himself out.

Now the foxy half dozen began to edge up. They were more than halfway to the pueblo. They were challenging each other and driving on that runner up ahead with the cornstalks.

The race grows hotter. The untrained and the unfit drop behind, but they keep on running in spite of the certainty that they can't win. Now a thin, leggy fellow begins to turn on the power. He widens the distance between himself and the foxy bunch, closes the interval between him and the man with the cornstalk bundle. Another runner accepts the challenge, forges up from the foxy group. He comes abreast of the leggy one; they battle for a hundred yards. Mr. Legs beats off the challenge. Now he has just one man to take, the guy with the cornstalks. That man, though, is unwilling to surrender his bundle, the baton of this race. He glances back, makes a valiant spurt.

But that lean Mr. Legs knows how to run. There's still half a mile to go. He encourages the leader to kill himself off. Makes sure no new challenger is coming up dangerously close from the rear. Then he moves faster, his stride long and smooth and determined. He begins to pass the leader. Reaches out eager hands. Takes the cornstalks! . . .

Mr. Legs really is running now. The taste of victory has him. The other foxy ones from behind turn on all they have, each man making his last desperate bid. But Mr. Legs still has what it takes. He keeps right on picking them up and putting them down too fast. The pueblo greets him, cheers him, runs to points of advantage to see what the final challengers can do about it. Then Mr. Legs bounds through his own door, and he's the man of the day.

At the Pueblo of Isleta, south of Albuquerque, Woods again succeeded where Parsons had been stymied. Isleta's native name ties the town to running, "Place of the Flint Kick-stick." Its races fit into an involved ritual which Parsons disclosed through one of the more ethically controversial episodes of American anthropology. She bought 140 paintings—some depicting running customs—which were sent to Washington clandestinely by an Isletan artist. His accompanying letters answered Parson's ethnographic queries and pleaded for anonymity, lest he be severely punished. When the paintings were published, and the artist's name revealed after his death, Isleta condemnation fell hard on his relatives.

In one letter the artist told how relay runners "are running for the sun to make the sun strong they call the sun road east to west." The races helped "clothe the sun," as runners moved back and forth, like bobbins on a loom, until one gained an entire lap to grab the dangling queue of the opposing man ahead.

Isleta's war chief set the date for the first spring race to coincide with the ditch cleaning. Traditionally the four-race series was held from mid-March to early April. At midnight before the first event, offerings were buried in a track which ran some 320 yards. (Charles Lummis secretly paced off its length from the Rio Grande River to the Santa Fe Railroad tracks.) Early on race day the track was scrupulously swept. After a morning race dance, the runners withdrew to the kiva, to stand and sing, "calling the sun." Undressing, their sides were painted white for Corn, red for War. A Town Chief watched for the first ray to penetrate the kiva's "sun hole" and strike its floor; he annointed the spot with pollen.

This was the signal to line the runners up in four rows, two east and two west. After race directors escorted them to respective ends of the track, their collective song stopped. With a shove of their bows, war chiefs prodded the starters into action.

Isleta women sweeping race track

Again Woods treated the event more as a track meet, but captured its verve as few ethnographers would dare:

> In order to win, a team must gain a complete lap, over and back. This is accomplished when the winning runner overtakes the losing team's man and slaps him on the back. In older times the practice was for the winner to seize the losing man by the hair or *chongo,* hence the name *Chongo* Race . . .
>
> Now the Turquoise man is reaching the west end just as the Pumpkin man makes it to the eastern starting line. That's half a lap lost. Now the Turquoise men in reality change from the pursued to the pursuer. All they have to do is to gain that other length of the course—about 200 yards. Eagerness spurs them into faster starts. The Pumpkin boys are getting disheartened.

It was as if the men became purified throughout their running. The loser, the last to grab the hair of the man ahead, exorcised the kiva, picking up butts of prayer cigarettes. Finally the runners conducted a ritual purge of the village, singing and drumming all the way.

Restricting Indian races to a single meaning or motivation is especially difficult for the most exotic track event of all, the "log running" of eastern Brazil. From the Payacú people in the south to the Araparýtiua near the mouth of the Amazon, over twenty Ge-speaking tribes have performed this pageant sport since origin times, and Westerners have chronicled it from the sixteenth century through today. Along the Tocantins River, the Krahô Indians claim that their ancestors, the sun and moon, invented the semi-religious game to play among themselves, and then passed it on to their human children.

Along roads hacked from the wilderness teams of relay runners toting logs that weigh from 100 to 200 pounds compete in races that climax in the spoke-patterned plazas of their thatch-roofed villages. The tracks extend in the four cardinal directions and are wide as country roads. Repaired every five years or so, some extend ten miles into the bush. Competing teams are made up of males from fifteen to fifty-five years old, although during role reversal ceremonies, women carry the men's logs and women's tumpline baskets hang from the men's foreheads. Pre-race preparations focus around carving rims to help the runners grip and balance the heavy logs on their shoulders. If fashioned from palm wood they are called *krowa,* if of hardwood, *para.* Body paint adorned the runners, with each tribe displaying favorite styles and colors. Tail-like hangings fell from their girdles, their long hair was fastened up with grass fans, and they wore cotton wristlets to prevent chafing as they shifted the log's weight.

This description comes from ethnographer Curt Nimuendajú, who worked among the Eastern Timbira in the 1930s. Naturally he was curious about the sport's origins. From the Timbira he heard nothing about mythological origins; the game had often been interpreted as a young man's test of marriageability, but Nimuendajú felt that while a worthy carry didn't hurt a man's chances at a wife, more had to be involved.

Another inquirer heard the running evolved from the need to bodily remove one's wife or comrades from harm's way in a fight; this could explain the log's weight which was equivalent to that of a human body. Nimuendajú noticed miniature logs decorated like women and featuring waxen breasts. However, he never received a satisfactory explanation whether it was sport, ritual, or test of strength. The Indians he queried provided contradictory and half-hearted answers, as if explanations were somehow beside the point.

For the full-blown race witnessed by Nimuendajú the teams gathered the night before to sing. On race day the challengers appeared at the track first; they were obliged to prepare the logs and bed them side by side on leaves. Their opponents announced their

arrival by trumpet blasts; once in sight the challengers sang and stamped their feet until the two teams were ready.

Forthwith four men from each team lift their own log to the first racer's shoulder, and he immediately dashes off in the direction of the village, followed and surrounded by a tumultuous troop of his fellows. The first choice is always one of the best runners, in order to have an encouraging start. When the two log bearers are running side by side, each has for his lane that side of the track on which his team had its log lying at the start of the race.

At once a mad chase starts in. Yelling and inciting the racers to greater efforts, blowing trumpets and ocarinas, the Indians with their waving grass ornaments bound deerlike to the right and left of the log-bearers' path, leaping over tufts of grass and low steppe bushes. After a distance of about a hundred and fifty meters, a fellow member runs up to the log bearer, who without stopping in his course dexterously twists his body around so as to transfer his load to his mate's shoulder and the race continues without the least interruption. Thus it goes on madly down the slopes of the hills in the torrid sunshine of the shadeless steppe,

Timbira log-runners, Brazil

across brooks and uphill again, in the burning, loose sand that unresistingly yields to the feet.

Soon the old folks and women carrying children are left behind, unless they have previously taken up a place ahead in order to see the racers dashing past somewhere farther on. Again and again a new substitute rushes up to relieve a racer as soon as his pace threatens to slacken. The spectators witness desperate efforts by the leaders and those who pique themselves on their reputation as log bearers. Nevertheless after a few kilometers the group of panting runners bathed in perspiration has diminished perceptibly. The cries urging one another on grow hoarse and forced, with an indescribably tortured ring. Nimble, light-footed maidens serve a draught of water to the racers from a gourd bottle as they run by, but no one is allowed to throw off the log for a stop and rest, no matter how far ahead his team may be.

At last the village appears on yonder height. With a last supreme exertion the runners force themselves up the sandy, worn incline. At this stage not a man is able to carry his load farther than thirty meters, so that there is a constant change of log bearers. But finally the houses of the boulevard are reached, and this street is followed to the door of the *vu'te* girl's house. Or, if

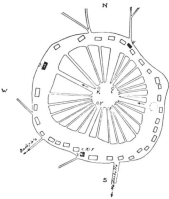

*Plan of Brazilian Indian village,
major roads are log-racing tracks*

Track for log-racing

the teams are composed of the plaza moieties, they take the nearest radial path to the plaza. At last the log is dropped with a thud . . .

And now we come to the feature that remains incomprehensible to the Neobrazilian and leads to his constantly ascribing ulterior motives to this Indian game: The victor and the others who have desperately exerted themselves to the bitter end receive not a word of praise, nor are the losers and outstripped runners subject to the least censure; there are neither triumphant nor disgruntled faces. The sport is an end in itself, not the means to satisfy personal or group vanity. Not a trace of jealousy or animosity is to be detected between the teams. Each participant has done his best because he likes to do so in a log race. Who turns out to be the victor or loser makes as little difference as who has eaten most at a banquet.

In the 1950s, British anthropologist David Maybury-Lewis let the Sherente tease him into joining their races. After jogging along for a

Brazilian Indian women log-running, 1968

spell, he drew near the log-bearer "like a tug approaching a liner"
and shouldered the huge baton:

> The ribbed bark of the palm trunk tore into my skin and it
> felt as if chips of bone were being flaked off every nobble in my
> shoulder. I had noticed that the Sherente carried the log almost
> behind the shoulder, resting it on the pad of skin at the junction
> of the neck and back. I tried to imitate them but I did not seem to
> have any pad there at all, or if I did it clearly was not sufficient.
> While I was thinking about it, I stumbled and nearly fell. It
> struck me that a fall with that log might cost me a broken limb
> . . . From then on I looked where I was going and stopped wor-
> rying about the pains in my shoulder. I was still jiggling the log
> about, wondering if I would ever get it comfortable, when a
> young man who had got his second wind dashed up and
> presented his shoulder. I felt that honour was satisfied and let
> him have the log. I trotted into the village among the log-racers
> and sat down on one of the racing logs which were beginning to
> clutter up the plaza in order to get my breath back.

Brazilian Indian woman log-runner, 1968

In the Brazilian states of Para and Maranhao log-racing apparently persists. "Among the Krīkatí and Pukóbye tribes," anthropologist Dolores Newton wrote me, "it is probably still a practice. I observed such races among them in 1968. They are among the five or so Timbira tribes still culturally functioning. When I was there in 1975 I saw no races, but there was no ceremony going on at the time, which is a *sine qua non* for such races. They *say* that this was not always the case—that in the 'good old days' there would be log races every morning at dawn. But who is to say at this point how much of such recollections is nostalgic hyperbole?"

The runners can't help bobbing and sidestepping rabbit brush and sprinkled juniper on the bumpy fourteen-mile jeep route which takes them to the lip of Acoma's basin. To the south the vista is barricaded by pastel cliffs. Westward looms Mesa Prieta, matted with juniper and pine. Above a layering of mesa planes to the north stands *Spi-nat,* where the Acoma say lives *Cakak,* the snow-bringer; we know it as 11,389-foot Mount Taylor.

Red streaks under his eyes, pouches for both Acoma and Zuni in hand, a runner drops onto the Pueblo's flat and grand approach, becoming a moving dot on the pencil-straight road toward the sandstone bulwark which has protected the "People of the White Rock" for nearly a millennium. The height of a forty-story apartment building, its scale is Olympian.

At the mesa foot, a runner veers off the blacktop to begin scrambling up the most ancient of six footpaths. Noticed by conquistadors in 1563, it was an obstacle course of toe-and-finger holds and ladders. After 1629 the trail next to it became known as the Camino de Padre when Father Juan Ramirez expanded it as his first step towards constructing San Estevan Mission. Then he conscripted Indians to haul vigas up it for his chapel from Mount Taylor, thirty miles off.

Acoma partook of the kick-stick racing tradition of the western Pueblos, as well as the "world-around" races of the east. In his retelling of an Acoma race yarn, the raconteur Charles Lummis has Coyote challenge Rabbit. After the requisite four-day waiting period, their race begins "around the four sides of the world." Coyote agrees to let Rabbit run underground, and finds him popping up his nose ahead at each corner until the finish line—whether he is the same Rabbit is the chuckle. Rabbit teases: "It is clear that big tails are not good to run with."

Lummis then told of an Acoma runner challenged to a ten-mile race by a Mexican on a burro. For four miles the Indian ran full tilt, but when he couldn't maintain the burro gained. Midway the trail entered the Malpais terrain and the Indian disappeared into a lava cave. As the Mexican passed, the Indian's twin came out to beat the burro by a hundred feet.

Atop Acoma I climb a weathered ladder to photograph the reception from a rooftop. Feather wands are slapped and the runners are blessed and thanked. Three miles to the north, sunlight breaks through colossal clouds turning 430-foot Enchanted Mesa into a golden pillar; Acoma tradition claims it as their former home. Beyond the little crowd below me the face of Acoma's cliff drops a sheer 350 feet; during the revolt it is believed that Father Lucas Maldonado was hurled to his death on the rocks below.

I have been unable to get much from these runners about their training or performance or the inner experience of the activity. Traditionally, Indians distinguished degrees and styles of running. When Don Talasyeva raced, Hopi onlookers teased him because his feet turned out so far they said it looked like he pinched his anus. Fred Kabotie told me that when his father carried 150 pound sacks of coal; "he would go sort of *tich-mama*, like a fox trot. Another word is *hena-nata,* not fast but not stopping. Fast runner pace is *a-nee-wa-dio-kta.* " The Nomlaki of California called their dodging movement, *t'eya*. David Maybury-Lewis said the Sherente of Brazil used the word *t'te'di* to indicate the desirable quality of tight and controlled speed.

Although these runners seemed uninterested in discussing their running with me, yesterday I overheard Bruce Gomez telling thirty-two-year-old Bruce Talawema of the Hopi crew how he admired Bill Rodgers' lightness of foot; to illustrate he dropped his open palm as if registering the warmth of a fire. Then I had a chance to talk with Talawema myself.

A personnel specialist for the Bureau of Indian Affairs in Washington D.C., Talawema was born in Hotevilla, but spent his maturing years in Indian boarding schools and the U.S. Marine Corps. He is a serious runner. Three years ago he did 2:33 in a Baltimore marathon. In 1975, 1976 and 1977 he ran the Boston marathon; his last time was 2:40. Talawema is a product of both Hopi and white coaching, so I was interested in his thoughts.

As a boy he had joined in the Basket Dance races, running four to eight miles in sand; the winners received woven plaques as prizes. "Running was something the elders used to preach to us," he said.

Runners at Acoma, San Juan Day, 1898

"Anytime you go somewhere on foot, you should try to run. It is a big part of our life. Even when you are old, as long as you can race or trot, at whatever pace, it makes you feel younger." He enjoys competition, running against the clock, but when I asked him to compare marathons with this experience, he said: "There's no comparison. There you're running for yourself. Here it's all tribal. We're running for the people. The other Pueblos are feeling the same thing. It is a matter of getting there and what we're carrying in terms of the message of peace and harmony and uniting as a people. Not to the extent that there might be another revolt, that's pretty much out of the question, but to find each other again. Time is not important to us, it's how we do it."

Nor did I need a stopwatch to cherish from this day the most vividly athletic image of the entire run. Clad only in striped shorts and running shoes as his legs gobbled the yards rising up Flower Mountain, Emmett Hunt Jr. ran as though his naked torso were hooked to a ski lift cable. His head didn't wobble, his feet never seemed to press upon the pavement, he powered with steady ease and grace. I've never witnessed running like it.

Runners approach Acoma, 7 August 1980

Zuni kick-stick runner, 1921

5.

Grants to Zuni
8 August

ON THE OLD ZUNI ROAD
A RUNNING PILGRIMAGE AND THE SACRED SHALAKO RACES
KICK-STICK RACE TRADITIONS
ON THE WAR GODS ROAD
PIMA COURIERS AND KICK-BALL PLAYERS
SHAMAN COACHES AND RUNNERS' WITCHERY
PAPAGO "SPEED RUNNING" VISIONS
PURIFICATION AT ZUNI

THE CLOUDS ABOVE Cibola National Forest redden as if reflecting an ignited river, burning out stars even as we watch. We hurtle south along New Mexico 53 searching in vain for Zuni runners to photograph against it before sunrise. Early last evening the Acomas bore the pouch twelve miles south, halting just short of Ice Caves. Watching from a parked car was Milton Sheyka, recreation aide and strategist of Zuni's part in the run. In the dusk stones were piled to mark the spot.

Yesterday storm squalls obliterated the Tafoya Canyon rim to the north, then massed on the freeway before Grants, turning day into night. Marble-sized hail and chilling rain lashed the runners. At the final underpass one boy collapsed into waiting arms, to be swaddled in blankets. Karl was robbed of another masterpiece: a rainbow curving down frame left, veins of white lightning shattering frame right, only his subjects were three minutes gone. We'd arranged with Sheyka to connect around 6:00 a.m. for a dawn shot. He'd seemed as idealistic about this historical replay as the Hopi crew, so I'm surprised when we can't find them, as clouds whiten and the skies above the spires of pines broaden with blue light.

High beams jiggling, the Zuni van swings at us. We both brake to talk through rolled-down windows; they've overshot the cairn. When we locate it, the photogenic moment is past. Their dozen runners bow heads on the two-lane road, blessing it with meal. Sheyka tells me: "We've given a girl, Danette Lementino, the honor of starting out. We're planning to get into the plaza near the church about one or two o'clock. Medicine men should be there to greet us." I detect a concern whether his people's enthusiasm will match his own.

Once an Indian trail, this road curves south then west around the Zuni Mountains. In the late 1500s it became a major Spanish *carretera* and was dubbed the Old Zuni Road when U.S. troops used it in the 1860s. Managing nearly five-mile laps, the Zunis zip across the Laguna Lava Flow; the road becomes a causeway across tarry ground which seems upturned as by some giant plow. Forty-two miles southwest of Grants they glide smoothly beneath 250-foot El Morro Rock. Over three and half centuries back Don Juan de Oñate carved his name in its sandstone base, starting a custom that continued until 1906 when the big rock's historical graffiti were deemed a national monument.

Twenty miles off is Zuni, the western frontier of New Mexico's Pueblos since the eighteenth century and today the largest. First the runners dip through the tree-shrouded hamlet of Ramah, where Navajos, Mormons, Zunis and cowboys have become a study in multi-cultural harmony. A man staggering onto the trading post porch with two cartons of dry goods stares as the runners swing through. Beyond the shade of Ramah's cottonwoods, they parallel the Rio Pescado while we hasten ahead to Zuni. "I have never heard from a Zuni the least reference to a historic event," commented anthropologist Alfred Kroeber over fifty years ago. Today we will have one little indication whether the Zuni have begun adding the white man's notion of public history to that timeless and private present.

Zuni kick-stick

Late in the afternoon of June 20, 1903, about sixty running men appeared near a ridge southwest of Zuni Pueblo. On their backs they carried bundles of sacred reeds, saplings and mud wrapped in corn husks. In their hands were live tortoises. They were completing a four-day running pilgrimage which had covered altogether 120 miles.

Stewart Culin, the scholar of Indian games, happened to be on hand, on a six-month buying trip for the Brooklyn Museum. He'd had his problems. The Zunis rushing to salute the runners had warned him back. He wasn't on hand to watch them change from running togs to dance costumes for the *Ko-kok-shi* rain celebration. He had the same difficulty getting clear explanations for Zuni's involved ritual life which would frustrate writer Edmund Wilson at the Shalako Festival some thirty years later. Culin did learn, however, that the contingent of runners represented most of Zuni's sacred and social brotherhoods. They had visited their sacred lake of emergence—about five miles north of St. Johns, Arizona—to harvest these raw ingredients for ritual paraphernalia.

Once their wanderings brought the ancient Zuni to the banks of the Zuni River—a tributary of the Little Colorado—their athletics incorporated the running mentioned so often in their mythology, the "messengers" and "fleet runners" who are "feared as by children now, for they were fierce and scourged people from their pathways to make room for those they guided." Running's role in their rituals today is largely symbolic. On the forty-ninth day of their Shalako Festival, six huge beaked and horned figures, impersonated by men with puppet frames on their shoulders, "race" south of town. Zunis

liken Shalako to our Christmas and New Year rolled into one renewal festival. Precariously the ten-foot Shalako totter back and forth as if fashioning a fabric, depositing prayer sticks at six pits on the open field. They are "trying their strength" for their duty as couriers of the gods, delivering prayers for rain all year. The Shalakos leave Zuni in a lineup ordered by a girl's foot race called *Molawia*, meaning "melons come," further linking their role to the hastening of crops.

Relay racing was the favored sport of eastern Pueblos, but here in the west the running events centered on competing teams booting sticks or balls around cross-country circuits. According to Frank H.

Race of the Zuni Shalako, 1896

Cushing, an early scholar adopted by the Zuni, their three-inch
sacred *tik-wa*, or kick-stick, was essential to the Zuni athlete's performance, ". . .were you to ask one of the runners to undertake the race
without his stick, he would flatly tell you he could not possibly do it.
So imbued with this idea are the Zunis that frequently, when coming
in from distant fields, and wishing to make haste, they cut a stick and
kick it ahead of them, running to catch up with it. . ."

Not that kick-stick was unknown in the east. The Tewa claim
that railroads and town obstructed their freedom to play the roving
game. Into this century the Keresan peoples played kick-stick. At
Jemez Pueblo Elsie Clews Parsons found the Summer Squash kiva

members kicking their blue-stick against the Winter Turquoise kiva men with their red stick on both the short mile race from the Jemez site of K'yapalo, as well as on a three-miler from Seytokwa—both old Jemez ruins marked by starting boulders. At Santa Ana Pueblo on San Juan Fiesta day, Turquoise and Squash runners began kicking their juniper sticks from the Turquoise kiva's north side to a cottonwood grove, yelling like kachinas bearing rain clouds. While some cut boughs for the dance, the rest raced home. The route followed the river-bank eastward, swung north, west and finally south for the homestretch into Santa Ana's plaza. The women refreshed them with water, as I'd witnessed at Zia and Jemez. At their kivas they tried punting their sticks onto the roof in one kick and booting them down the ladder wall with a second kick for good luck. No prize or recognition awaited the runners. It was for rain; as an Acoman told Leslie White, "the kachinas use kick-sticks when they come bringing the rain. If you watch the water coming down off a mesa during a rain, you will see that it does not flow evenly; it comes in spurts. That is because the kachinas are running along, kicking their (kick-sticks)."

Acoma's seven kivas were also pitted against each other, four men per team if the distance was eight to ten miles, two or three for the shorter course. They carved four sizes of stick, but the largest was rarely used since its weight "made the boys run too fast." Acoman runners admired the hummingbird as a "messenger" who could impart swiftness to them. Before races, the stakes—arrows, buckskins, belts, leggings and bows—were heaped in the plaza. Ground isinglass was rubbed around the sticks to distinguish them with one and two rings each. Each team assigned a man to keep track of where the sticks fell. Unlike Santa Ana's runs, a west-south-east-north circuit was followed; afterwards the war chief prayed over the sticks, then deposited them in shrines or cornfields as rain offerings.

It was at Zuni, however, that kick-stick racing was most venerated in myth, elaborated in ritual, and enthusiastically played as sport by males from five to fifty years of age. On summer evenings one might see twenty to thirty boys kicking sticks on the southern hill; Zunis stretched the game's season to eight months. Before the

Zuni existed, the mischievous brother-gods who transformed themselves into great warriors at will were chronic kick-stick players. Runaway youngsters were said to stumble upon their kick-sticks out in the desert and play with them. Zuni folklore attests to the sport's antiquity. Among their kick-stick stories is the matrimonial race for the hand of a village priest's daughter. Using magic given him by kachina helpers, a handsome spirit-man wearing a frog skin draws rain to the western approach to Zuni, hiding his opponent's kick-stick so he can win the girl. So imbued were the Zuni with the tie between racing and rain that when Zuni farmers chanced upon mud-balls in a gully they considered them kick-sticks of the gods, to be buried around their irrigation systems to tempt water spirits to play there.

Their season for kick-stick, or *tikwane*, opened four days after the April full moon, when planting was over or between putting in the wheat and corn. From rooftops war priests called for all six kivas to ready their players. North, south and nadir kivas ran on behalf of the elder War God; east, west, and zenith kivas stood in for younger War God. Early every morning the runners exercised; the priests

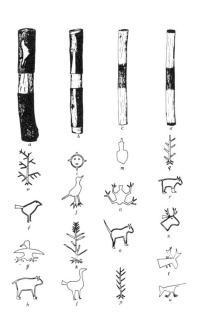

Zuni clan symbols carved into kick-sticks for identification during races: a: Macaw. b: Yellow Wood. c: Older Brother Bow Priest. d: Younger Brother Bow Priest. e: Dogwood. f: Raven. g: Eagle. h: Badger. i: Sun. j: Turkey. k: Corn. l: Crane. m: Pumpkin. n: Frog. o: Coyote. p: Tansy Mustard. q: Tobacco. r: Bear. s: Deer. u: Chaparral Cock.

planted six prayer plumes about two miles from the village on both sides of the track now consecrated as the "road of the gods of war."

Before the afternoon races, the men washed their hair with yucca root—with a second cleansing later. From now on they only ate *hewe*—a paste of tissue-thin unleavened bread and water. Shovelling the sticks past the prayer plumes, the runners stretched their arms to breathe in the flying power of *sho'kapiso*, the hawk. At the finish their kick-sticks flew into the river, to float to the homeland of the Council of the Gods.

Religious solemnity also attended kick-stick racing among the sixteen Zuni clans. Runners had maternal clan symbols painted on their chests, paternal on their backs. Now the stage was set for hotly contested, long-distance kick-stick games which once vied with races among the Tarahumara, Hopi and Taos peoples as the best documented Indian game. From the 1880s through the 1930s, outsiders thrilled to these contests around a twenty-five mile course, the runners pursued by a movable stadium of mounted fans. Unlike the earlier races for collective well-being, the supernatural tone of these runs was intensely partisan.

On retreats runners might plant prayer sticks and shell, tobacco, and meal offerings at special shrines. At Owl Spring, one aspirant petitioned a nesting owl, "They are going to run a kick-stick race today and my grandmother told me to ask you what to do." Replied the bird, "Pull a feather from my left wing and carry it when you run . . . my sleeping will overcome them and they will be too tired to race." Running homeward from such visitations, "without speaking above a whisper," runners stayed keen to any roosting bird—owls especially—which indicated they were being witched. They were also alert to auguries of victory: lightning, shooting stars, red-shoulder hawks, McGillivray's warblers, hummingbirds, or the sound of rushing water.

In 1890, Frederick Hodge launched his eminent ethnographic career by writing about a Zuni kick-stick run. He was staggered by the stakes, silver belts, bracelets, shell necklaces, horses, sheep, blankets, piled high in the plaza beside the church. All night before

Four Zuni runners, 1890

the event runners kept vigil, singing, praying, and offering food to the War Gods and the spirits of dead runners. For training they ran in the early morning, and abstained from coffee lest it distend their stomachs. Toward afternoon they donned white or red cotton running shorts to identify their team, knotted their hair over their forehead, and tucked in an arrowhead for speed. Throughout the race an old woman might hold a cherished old jar, decorated with deer and hummingbird designs for speed. Near its "feeding hole" hung a deer horn carved like an oaken kick-stick. To both teams it lent good luck, and sometimes it crowned the pile of wagered goods. (For intra-kiva races, an old woman would be brought to the ceremonial chamber to pray for its players. Utensils of the hearth piled around her would render the opponents warm and the brooms would make them tired.) Finally the racers might slip two shell beads into their mouths, one to drop as a sacrifice at the start, the other at mid-point.

Four to a team, the racers staggered themselves so as not to block their teammates' view. Their sticks were distinguished by one or two bark rings, and lead runners first laid them in the trough behind the toes. In Hodge's day a mounted priest "opened the road" with a handful of cornmeal.

As the race commenced, Hodge was impressed by the long casts, thirty feet high and at times a hundred feet long. Inevitably the sticks got snagged or lost. Forbidden to use their hands, the men dug at them with hardened bare feet. Keeping abreast of the teams were nearly 300 horsemen, galloping close to harangue laggers, caking the sweating runners with dust.

They roamed counter-sunwise, over the southern hills, turning east to Thunder Mountain and following it to the Zuni River. Holding to the mesas along the northern rim, they forded the stream two miles west of town and came home through sandy cornfields. Approaching the finish line riders unravelled rippling bolts of calico. Here the runners could pick up their sticks and break for the plaza. Leaping over the piled stakes, they put the kick-sticks to their mouths, inhaling their "breath of life" before tearing for home. There the sticks lay in a basket until the following day when they were buried six inches below ground in an arroyo, to be washed away by the desired rains. Hodge estimated the race took two hours and covered around twenty-five miles; forty-two years later Elsie Parsons witnessed another race that only went eight miles and took an hour and a quarter.

By 1934, when Roy Keech wrote what may be the final eye-witness report of such a run, Navajos were in attendance and the bets included Pendleton blankets from Oregon, silk shawls from central Europe and stockings. When two gamblers agreed on a bet their stakes were lashed together and silver coins in beaded pouches topped the pile. First the teams marched to a field south of Zuni's "center of the world" shrine to pray. Their forelocks were bound with yucca strips, their kick-sticks were identified with one or two ochre bands. To point out lost sticks, a horseman carrying a willow wand tipped with a white feather was attached to the teams. As Keech told it:

> Probably five hundred gayly attired horsemen followed, besides many runners not fortunate enough to possess mounts. South the two teams ran, following their sticks, with the leaders continually changing. First they ran down a lane between planted fields toward the great green and white mesa south of Zuni. Then through open country they went and across arroyos, swerving to the east, to the foothills. Then up and down little hills and through small valleys and ravines, just to the west of To-wa Yallon-i, their sacred mountain, they ran, raising clouds of dust all along the way. And the cavalcade thundered behind. Now they circled a bit to the west. Now they turned north and travelled through a long lane fenced with barbed wire. Now, far to the west again they ran, showing against retreating scarp cliffs of red sandstone below and yellow above. What a picture! Through sand, stones, rabbit-bush, and cacti, over hills and dipping into ravines and more arroyos, they rushed toward their goal. On they ran, never stopping to catch their breath, or to wet their parched lips. The great body of horsemen shouted, yelled, and yipped.
>
> Now the cavalcade again circled to the south, as they divided into two groups, each following its favorite team of runners. The Governor's team was behind now, but gaining slowly. Excitement ran high. Again the two teams circled, to enter the pueblo from the south. The Governor's team was gaining fast. The

women and girls and children on the housetops squealed in their delirious expectation; for their fathers, brothers, sweethearts, and husbands had bet heavily, and the winners would divide generously with their womenfolks.

Neck and neck the two teams were racing now! Up the village street they came from the south. Then the opposing team kicked its stick into the Zuni River, and the Governor's team lost!

The race had started at five o'clock and ended at seven. This is the Zuni method of working up an appetite for the evening meal, after a day in the corn or hay field. There remained only the dividing of the plunder among those who had bet on the winning team.

Zuni kick-stick runners, 1921

Three hundred miles west of Zuni flourished a kick racing tradition with Olympic overtones. While running in the Piman and Yuman speaking worlds played its part in warfare, communication and vision-seeking, their inter-village kick-ball games also seemed to function as surrogate warfare and a mechanism for distributing surplus food.

Along the Gila and Colorado Rivers girls and boys were encouraged to run from childhood, in both kick-ball and relay racing. As Piman boys grew to manhood, they ran down deer. A Papago hunting recitation opens: "Hither and yon they ran. This way they ran and killed the deer. There kept barking the comrade. There (the deer) fell and thrashed about. Then did a shaman run up. He moved the deer and laid him with his head to westward." Once chased to earth, the animal was smothered and its prized black tail cut off.

In traditional times every Papago's village's "Keeper of the Meeting" had a personal messenger, his "Leg." Infirm leaders might also be assigned helpers named "Eyes," "Ears," or "Voice." Laying the Keeper's fire, the "Leg" sat behind him ready to carry messages of war and challenges for the inter-village athletic events usually scheduled for autumn.

Instead of sticks, however, croquet-size balls were kicked around twenty to thirty mile circuits. Formed from stone or mesquite or palo verde wood, they were coated with creosote gum. Before the large wintering groups broke up for summer's planting and foraging, runners and their families proposed a match to the "game leader." In turn the idea was broached to the council, whereupon the prime runners were evaluated to see if the odds were in the village's favor.

All summer the women cleared the practice areas of thorns, and trainees took twenty-five mile runs into the hills each day. Prospective team runners drank a little water before noon, and abstained from meat, honey, or cactus syrup. Veteran players whose toenails were thick as horn critiqued the runners' technique and rehearsed the running-song cycles night and day. The athletes cast their own spells, blowing smoke toward their opponents' village, incanting, "You are not a great runner, I can beat you."

Yuman runner, Colorado River

Papago runner

The awaited match arrived in late fall between the harvest and departure from the summer camp. The guest team brought their relatives and supporters; gifts and food were soon passing hands in large quantity. These meets were also contests between shaman-coaches. Before gametime spell-makers scrutinized the track to check that no opposing shaman had pounded a notched stick to render his men invisible. The stakes were also exorcised. With song power and public performances such as sword swallowing, medicine men "raced for us with their tricks all night."

One renowned shaman, Something Laid There Loose, used his powers from the morning star to shoot off a chunk of rainbow to place above his runner so opponents couldn't reach the lad. Another runner, visited by a hawk spirit, began to grow feathers from his elbows and wrists. The magic-making was assisted by the songs and spells for which Papagos were renowned.

PAPAGO RUNNING SONGS

At the edge of the flat land.
Here I come out and run.
On top of the mountain.
Here I come out and run.
Evening falls while I run.

I come forth running,
I come forth running,
Bearing a cloud on my head,
I come forth running.

I speed up my kick-ball,
Over the flat ground it flies.
Between the spreading branches
It settles down.

The hawk laid out the racetrack;
The hawk laid out the racetrack;
On it the man won. Ah!
Wild, the man came here;
Wild, the man came here;
A hawk's heart he won. Ah!

Evening is falling!
Like an eagle I move
Back and forth.
Morning is standing!
Like a hawk I run
Back and forth.

As further precaution against devilry, players were hidden from sight until the last minute. Anthropologist Ruth Underhill mentions a race whose entrants were delivered by horseback a half-mile away to escape contamination, and crowds were kept a hundred feet back—safe range from conjuring. Even so shamans managed to work their wiles, like the Pimas who scored lines across the route of their Maricopa opposition so they would believe they had encountered deep canyons; or they would sprinkle the Maricopas with reeds of water to "drown" them. Whenever one Maricopa came abreast of his Pima opponent the man breathed his way; suddenly the Maricopa felt as though the air had been sucked from his lungs. Another Pima on the sidelines touched him with a switch and he seemed to be stunned by a club. He began to give up until one of his shamans flicked him with a rope. He spurted ahead just as the overly-confident Pimas were reaching for the stakes.

Back at the village onlookers raced relays and played pick-up kick-ball. A run could last hours—one 1893 game started at noon and wound up at 8:00 p.m. Men ran so hard that death was not unknown. On the Papago reservation, reports Bernard L. Fontana,

Papago kick-ball race

121

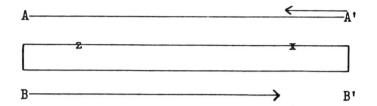

*Pima relay track: If a runner from A outruns runner from B so that A's relief run-
ner, A^1, meets B on the course, a mark is put at the point of his meeting (x). If A^1
maintains his lead, his relief man (the next runner from A) should meet B^1 on the
course, and the judges place a second mark at the point (z). If team A gains steadily,
the two marks, x and z, approach each other, and finally meet about the middle of
the course. Because team A will then have gained an entire lap, it is then declared the
winner. Evenly matched teams might run a single race all day long.*

Painted Papago racer, 1925

a shrine was placed where one runner breathed his last and dropped. When they reappeared around sunset, the racers cupped their hands over their mouths, calling shrilly. With peculiar abruptness and no ceremony the winnings were turned over, the camp disbanded. When women of the Pima and Papago held their races, they used sticks to toss ahead little batons of cactus rib.

For the Papago, running played a part in more transcendental pursuits. "Am I not the runner. . ." says the speechmaker at the Saguaro Wine Feast, celebrating the tribe's new year. He goes on to describe a dream-like run toward a rainhouse full of winds, clouds and seeds. This seems a model for the Papago speed-running on the beaches of the Gulf of California, which occurred at the finale of a week-long pilgrimage for salt from Arizona to the ocean.

For years men trained in anticipation of this experience. After arriving at the salt sloughs, the pilgrims made offerings to the ocean. "Be favorable to me," they pleaded, "be smooth. Let me run and see what I shall see." At this they ran twenty miles to a headland and back, straining for a life-guiding vision.

They ran so arduously that some of them died. Underhill reported that when one runner saw white cranes ahead they seemed to be men setting his pace. Then he knew he was fated to become a great kick-ball racer. Another runner saw a mountain slowly revolving before him. The songs he composed about it won him prominence in the skipping dance. A third runner heard a voice: "The sea shaman wants to see you." Suddenly he disappeared and for the next four years inhabited a cave and learned sacred songs. When he returned home, he had been given up for dead. His property had been burnt after his funeral. However, that vision made him a renowned medicine man and he earned back all his losses.

When I've wandered around Zuni it has usually been in the dark, stumbling across the December snow from one ritual house to another during Shalako. I inevitably get lost in my search for warmth and my fear of missing something. At Shalako, you learn, you're always missing something. But it is host night at Zuni, so you always can exchange the crisp night for the overheated, brilliantly decorated shelter of the new homes which are being consecrated during the spirits' visitation.

This midday the community fragments out like a bordertown. At its core stand the rock-and-adobe remains of the Zuni village known as *Halona,* or "Red Ant Place." It suggests an Algerian Casbah; you sidle circumspectly around crumbling masonry corners, piles of twisted juniper and piñon firewood, clothes lines and beehive-shaped ovens, like tip-toeing through someone's living room. Sur-

Zuni runners near Ramah, 8 August 1980

rounding it are the decentralized, government-built houses and fenced, single-family lots of twentieth century Zuni. I'd almost rather be here at night. We pass a New York hustler with crayoned "Will Buy" sign stuck under his windshield wiper, making a killing on clandestine jewelry deals.

With relief we locate the old sector and park in an undistinguished, dusty opening beside the weed-clotted courtyard of the church. It is actually fabled ground, known as *Tehwitta-Tlanna*, Zuni's main plaza where dances are held and at one time the arena for launching kick-stick races. Here was where Hodge had marvelled at the rich pile of wagered goods.

An elderly man in short sleeves sidles over to find out what two white guys with cameras and notepads are about. He's fifty-year-old Louis Tsethlikai. Before joining the paratroops he was an ardent kick-race player and believes he ran in the very last one, around 1949. By then Navajos had participated and Zuni cupboards hung with silver bracelets and concho belts they won from them. The Zuni also challenged U.S. soldiers stationed at Fort Wingate. Tsethlikai couldn't explain kick-racing's demise, but in the van this morning the Zuni team confided to me that the witchcraft and gambling associated with the sport had aggravated family feuds. When they mentioned kick-racing it was with palpable fear, as if the tradition had somehow become ugly and destructive.

Tsethlikai's uncles were top kick-stick players who taught him it was the War Gods' game. As young boys they had kicked sticks around cornfields as they drove off crows. They'd taught him to steer clear of greasy foods before running, "and of course alcohol. We'd wear only trunks, and the arrowhead in the headband. We had about six races a year, mostly on Saturdays. We'd start about three or four in the afternoon, breathing through our noses because the horses kicked up all that dust. But we also used to run and pray every day. In morning I went for a sprint, then about 4:00 in the afternoon I just ran and ran, from here to Caliente and back, about twenty-eight miles in three or four hours."

This sort of performance developed from habituation and hard training. "In springtime we'd start walking barefooted," Tsethlikai told me, "and get used to it until the skin was a quarter-inch thick and you could run on glass and it wouldn't hurt you. And we'd heat treat them. My uncle showed me how to build a fire and put motor oil on my feet and warm them up. Gets thick as the sole of your shoe."

Since morning Gallup radio forty miles due north has been heeding Sheyka's wishes to announce the incoming runners. From the crowded look of the rooftops, his anxieties about community interest are unfounded. I want a better vantage point and climb to the Brain Kiva roof, hopping to the roof of the Dogwood Clan house. Down below War Priest Morris H. Laahty, a portly man in crew cut, strews a cornmeal finish line north-south across the plaza, then another line toward the expected runners. Gravely he waits, two immense eagle-wing plumes crossed in his hand.

Before noon the first runner, local track star Kenny Bobelu, lopes in with the others following at half-minute intervals, each of them receiving respectful applause. One by one they are blessed by Laahty, sweeping his feathers up and down their bodies as if picking up unseen forces, then slapping them together with finality. His prayers over, hundreds of men on the rooftop and below spit behind them. The runners have been cleansed of any evil they might have picked up outside Zuni. Their fellow villagers have also expelled threatening outside influences, perhaps with the same impulse that they killed Father Juan del Val during the Rebellion. The runners are reintegrated into Zuni. The unkempt townscape is suddenly replaced in my awareness by the survival of Zuni metaphysics. This remains the legendary "Middle Place," despite the trailer homes and banged-up automobiles. There is still an altar in the center of Zuni, they say, holding a stone in which beats the heart of the world.

The runners hover over Lt. Governor Theodore Edaakie as he opens the pouch, and as abruptly as a kick-race finale, it is all over. Among the runners handshakes and embraces pass around. Sheyka is handing water to one as I walk up; he is glowing. "They came," he says, while around him people trickle back to work. "They understood what we were doing."

First runner into Zuni, 8 August 1980

Navajo racers

6.

Window Rock to Ganado
9 August

HOPIS ACROSS NAVAJOLAND
RUNNING TEACHINGS OF TALKING GOD:
THE NAVAJO "DAWN RUNNERS"
APACHE BOOT CAMP: TRAINING GUERRILLA RUNNERS
CHANGING WOMAN'S DAUGHTERS: PUBERTY RUNNING RITES
THE INCAN *WARACIKOY* DOWNHILL ORDEAL
"POWER RUNNING" AMONG THE YUROK
ARRIVAL AT GANADO

IT'S TOO EARLY in the morning for this capital of America's most populous and expansive Indian reservation to sizzle with Navajo energy, as scattered families within a hundred-mile radius wheel their flashy pickups here for a Saturday-in-town. For the Hopi runners streaking along Arizona 264, however, probably too many Navajos are awake already.

Yesterday, on the dirt roads between San Luis, Torreon, White House and Crownpoint they enjoyed a private, raucous camaraderie. This morning they continue to greet each other with face-fulls of water, but seem edgy to get through. The lifestyle of the spread-out Navajo and Apache cultures contrasts with the Pueblo impulse to cluster and centralize; this is also a reflection of their divergent tribal personalities. In 1868 the Navajos were given a huge land base, virtually surrounding the Hopi's three mesas. A live-and-let-live policy prevailed until 1962 when a federal court decreed that the Hopi owned 640,000 acres immediately around the mesas, with some adjacent lands designated as a Joint Use Area. Twelve years later, however, this territory was further divided. With 5,000 Navajos slated for eviction, old and deep distrusts were aroused.

The Hopi seem to run a double gauntlet: first through enemy territory their runners long ago penetrated in search of Navajo materials to take home and convert into war magic, second, through the boomtown rawness of Window Rock with its parking lots, motels and gas stations scraped into the rusty desert. With relief they pass the St. Michaels Mission turnoff and roll through high ponderosa groves towards Cross Canyon, still steaming with morning burnoff.

But Navajos are not so easily avoided on their own turf. In a clearing off the road a few lingering men watch us and warm their backs at the embers of a Squaw Dance bonfire, the colloquial name for an all-night Enemy Way curing ritual. Two miles further celebrants are exiting from a smoke-blackened peyote tipi. At a change point on their way to Ganado a Hopi walks off the strain of his lap. A Navajo flatbed crawls to pass and two boys, lying on their stomachs behind the cab, yell, "What are you running for?" With a shy, feisty whisper, the Hopi replies, "For the people."

Tricentennial runners near Window Rock, 9 August 1980

Portion of navajo sandpainting depicting mythological runner's foot and hand print.

Even the Pueblos admit that movement and Navajos are synonymous. Unlike the Hopi, the Zuni have usually found a place for Navajo visitors and athletes. While they recall always winning at kick-stick races, Zuni mythology credits the Navajo with being superior runners. At the beginning, when only Zunis and Navajos had eyes strong enough to stare straight at the sun, the famous twins, Morning Star and Evening Star, first offered corn to Indians. Morning Star wanted a race to allocate its distribution, so the Zuni, Acoma and Navajo put up their fastest men.

Morning Star broke an ear of corn into three chunks. Finishing first, the Navajo got the tip, the Acoma won the middle, and the Zuni took the butt end. Morning Star was concerned, but his brother reassured him, "It is well. The Navajo is the swiftest runner. He will always be moving from place to place. He will not be able to take care of much corn." So it is today that the Navajo, unlike the stationary Pueblos, are ever shifting between their summer and winter homesteads.

Running was a required course in schooling for war, work and spiritual readiness within the Athabaskan-speaking world. Among the Navajo, their practice of running at dawn exuded that extra poetry in motion which colors their liturgies and world view; for the Apache there was a grimmer focus on running as survival training.

Three days earlier I'd interviewed an eighteen-year-old Navajo who had trained to run before sunrise. At Zia I'd caught a lift in the homey VW bus of Janet and Sam Bingham, teachers at Rock Point Community School in the center of Navajo land. They'd brought Rex Lee Jim, born in the Canyon de Chelly region and raised to run by his grandfather, Hosteen Yellowhair. Rex proved eager to talk about his people's running customs.

"My grandfather told me that Talking God comes around in the morning, knocks on the door, and says, 'Get up, my grandchildren, it's time to run, run for health and wealth.' " Thus his grandfather would roust Rex before dawn. Though Yellowhair is now dead, even these days when his father wakens him Rex can expect cold water in the face if he doesn't get moving.

For Navajo runners, Talking God, the "grandfather of the Gods," is the archetypal coach. Travelling on rainbows and sunbeams from his home of corn pollen, there is something of the Zen master about him. He will communicate only by gestures. He's known to tease those he guides toward self-fulfillment and the Navajo ideals of enterprise, courage and quick mind. Running helps to root those virtues and direct one towards an industrious life.

"My grandfather used to tell me stories how the gods reward you if you run early in the morning," Rex said. Among them was the challenge of the Navajo gods to the sacred twins, five days after their birth. When the deities won, the babies were whipped with boughs of mountain mahogany. The twins practiced for four days, raced them again and won, and scourged the gods in return. Talking God is said to have clapped his hands in delight.

Rex was about four years old when his grandfather began waking him and his brother about 4:30 a.m. "We'd have to beat the sunrise. Usually you run to the east, every day or so making about a hundred yards more until you're running about four miles in all. Usually my grandfather would gather some sagebrush and have us boil it, drink it fast, and start running hard so that by the time you get several yards you threw up and cleaned your body. No breakfast until we get home for fried bread and all that."

"In the winter," Rex grimaced, "you'd roll in the snow first. Then you just take off, and after a while you get so hot. I did it once but I'll never do it again." Other Navajos have described this freeze-bath as mandatory. During winter's second snow, always colder than the first, youngsters would enter the morning dark wearing only moccasins and breechcloths, take a short sprint, then shake

Rex Lee Jim, Navajo runner, 1980

snow from tree limbs onto their bodies. Later in life men claimed immunity from the weather because they had rolled in the snow as boys. It staved off laziness, made the eyes clear and the body strong.

Left-Handed, a Navajo whose life history was published by anthropologist Walter Dyk as *The Son of Old Man Hat*, told of running to a body of icy water. ''If there was thick ice on top of the water I'd get a stick or a piece of rock, break the ice, take off my moccasins, and jump in. I'd stay in the icy water as long as I could stand it, turning over and over, hollering and screaming so as to develop a good voice. Then I'd get out and put on my moccasins and start for home. While I'd be running on my way my body would be covered with a thin coat of ice, cracking all over me and my cock. My cock would be almost frozen. That was the hardest thing; I sometimes couldn't stand it. Before going in the hogan, I'd roll in the snow once more.''

Daily exposure, enforced by parents, could overcome deep-seated fears. Once beyond his hogan's security, one Navajo dawn runner slowed to a walk and finally sat on the ground until first light. Then he hustled home, pretending to be out of breath. But his folks caught on and made him get back out; soon he was not afraid to run in pitch-black mornings.

Left-Handed described packing his moccasins with sand to toughen his feet, ''so as to be able to run anywhere . . . even though the snow was twelve inches deep or more I could run through it as though there were nothing on the ground.'' He would take a mouthful of water and hold it as he ran, breathing only through his nose to build his wind.

Rex recalls that on the run east his grandfather made him yell. Once before he started, twice en route, and finally, ''the fourth time when I stopped at 'the shaping place.' You yell: *oo-way-witch-awatcha*. You make the *o* really long, and the *way* really long, one after another.'' Other Navajos describe running with icicles in their mouths. Talismans might be carried. Rex tied an arrowhead behind his ear or gripped a ''small, bean-like thing'' for speed on long distances. On his body he might smear an unguent, ''pollen shaking off,'' mixed from lard and corn pollen which had been rubbed onto bird or animal skins. Bear fur medicine toughened your muscles, whereas if it had soaked up mountain lion fur or eagle skin you became fast. Rex also learned some of Talking God's songs—the mountain lion, antelope and deer songs—known collectively as "Leg Songs," which he sang while running long distances.

Navajo runners were careful about what they ate. In the Endurance Chant myth, Coyote says to Big Monster, "One who eats rare game can run fast, but what can you expect of a person who eats worms, grasshoppers, and lizards! No wonder you cannot race." Other pieces of running lore suggest, however, that little meat was eaten before a run; Navajos sometimes consumed a ceremonial mush.

Rex's morning routine was interrupted at a halfway point where he and his brother performed another ritual. "Where you stop, you must run around a bush clockwise, and then you press the skin down to your muscles and punch them hard. If you have someone with you, you lay down and sort of massage his muscles, and then he would do you. We call it 'shaping' your body." Sometimes they used an eagle feather to induce further vomiting.

Running back, punctuated by four more drawn-out yells, ended with fanfare too. "You have to run around the hogan the way the sun goes, and turn four times, and if you have corn pollen hold it to your chest and breathe deeply four times." Then the boys bolted through their hogan door.

"There's hardly anyone who runs in the mornings now," Rex believes, although a 1936 survey showed over a half of the Ramah Navajo parents still made their boys roll in the snow. "I definitely would teach it to my children," he adds. "It is good for your fitness and your reputation, and it provides more contact with the gods. If you say, 'Oh, I'll run in the morning,' then you have to, or you're lying to the gods. It's good when you're looking for horses. It's a great feeling if you're known to be really fast and they say, 'Catch that horse.' "

These days Rex runs occasionally at noon, following a pattern where Navajos past the age of eleven or twelve graduated from dawn running to lengthier runs at midday in a sunwise direction. As was once the habit of Yana Indian youth in central California, Rex still

Navajo runners, c. 1910

takes off near sunset, "when I give myself a sort of challenge, running east away from the sun to try and outrun my shadow."

Against the lyrical Navajo style, the Spartan approach of the Apache regimen sounds like boot camp. Focused largely on stretching the pain and endurance thresholds of its eight to twelve-year-old conscripts, Apache training prepared boys for war and a safe escape the Apache way, on foot, often at a clip, and possibly all alone. They began working with their youngsters when character and physique were still malleable. Running was paramount among the methods of stamping tribal values and goals upon the young. Theirs was a pitiless world view.

"My son," instructed the Apache father, "you know no one will help you in this world . . . You must run to that mountain and come back. That will make you strong. My son, you know no one is your friend, not even your sister, your father, or your mother. Your legs are your friends; your brain is your friend; your eye-sight is your friend; your hair is your friend; your hands are your friends; you must do something with them."

Among the Chiricahua Apache a boy's father introduced him to this survival school. "Be up before daylight and run up the mountain," he would command. "Be back before daylight. You must do it, and I'm going to make you do it . . . I am going to train you so that when you get to be a few years older you will be almost as good as any man. Your mind will be well developed. Your legs will be developed so nobody can outrun you."

Before the boys assumed full warriorhood, this hardening process became institutionalized into what anthropologist Morris Opler terms the "novice complex." They entered a pecking order which initially entailed dunking themselves in iced-over creeks, crashing through sharp ice without being allowed to dry by the fire, and carrying packs on their backs while running. They were commanded to punch tree limbs, to fight each other until they cried, to leap at high green branches and wrench them out, to keep rolling a ball of snow until allowed to stop.

Eating habits were scrutinized; they grew used to empty bellies. They were lectured to stay away from women and smoke. Instead, they had to run constantly and take sweat baths. Trainers bragged about their boys and pitted them against each other. One demonstrated his student's maneuverability by shooting at his feet with live ammunition while the boy ran down a hillside.

Tougher training followed, as the recruits were lined up, given mouthfuls of water, and inspected after a four-mile trot to make sure they could spit it out. For a finale a two-day run without food or long halts might be assigned on a prearranged route. When they had proven themselves adequately self-sufficient, the young men—about sixteen years old—joined a series of four war parties, each a rung up on the ladder to warriorhood. At first they were only allowed to touch their bodies with scratching sticks and drinking tubes. Now running became the foundation for wilderness orienteering and dodging techniques used on platoon-size raids in the field.

137

The Apache specialty, hit-and-run warfare, often found men stranded from their comrades, so everyone packed their own food. They learned to travel across flats at night and to rest by day. Aware the Mexicans and Indians would hunt for them first in deep shade, they avoided stopping beneath trees when the sun was up, hiding instead in tall grass or brush. From hilltops they sought out green watering holes, but only visited them after dark.

On their first two forays, novices followed a scenario. They must not look around or behind them; instead of eating guts, they should consume lungs for lightness and swiftness. On their second raid they refrained from sleeping; when they rested rock pillows kept them from dozing. Their food should be eaten cold—to keep their teeth from dropping out later in life. Morning and night they should run, run, run. They were encouraged to dash up hills near camp and urinate on trees and howl like coyotes to stay smart and out of trouble. Homeward bound they must not sit lest a "heaviness" overcome their fellow warriors.

Novices noticed older warriors singing "leg songs" to overcome tiredness and painting "wind tracks" on their moccasins for lightness. Some owned the sort of exceptional power which helped Apaches leave Fort Grant at dawn and run to Fort Apache by midafternoon. This training enabled men to regroup after an ambush, for it was generally the getaway after a raid, preferably at night during a full moon, when those injunctions about self-dependence became a reality.

Even after they had access to horses, the Chiricahua preferred making war on foot. During his guerrilla strikes into Mexico, Geronimo would strike hard and fast, then disperse his men with prearranged rendezvous points three days hence. Their scattered tracks stymied pursuing Mexican military or U.S. cavalry. Geronimo remembered travelling forty miles a day, but one of his soldiers recalled it was closer to seventy-five miles, carrying three days' rations and staying on the move fourteen hours including short meal stops.

From boyhood through old age, constant running developed

fighters with the kind of phenomenal endurance which drew the following backhanded compliment from veteran Indian fighter, Colonel R. I. Dodge. Unaware that the Indian training was tougher than that of his troops, and neglecting to mention that Indians were fighting for their motherland, Dodge wrote, ''The tenacity of life of an Indian, the amount of lead he will carry off, indicates a nervous system so dull as to class him with brutes rather than men. . .I myself have seen an Indian go off with two bullets through his body, within an inch of his spine, the only effect of which was to cause him to change his gait from a run to a dignified walk.''

While running in these physical programs was guided by mythological precepts, its function was eminently practical: to turn out hard fighters. However the running segment in rite-of-passage rituals for young Navajo and Apache women personifies the spirit of Changing Woman (Navajo) and White Painted Woman (Apache).

Although Talking God, overseer of well-madeness, is credited with originating the Navajo girl's puberty ceremony known as *Kinaalda*, its massaging and running features were to symbolically fashion the girl in body and soul as strong, upright and beautiful as Talking God's protégé, Changing Woman. During the four-day rite, when extended family and friends honor her first menstruation, the girl might run up to three times a day, just as dawn lightens the sky. She runs to the east, from 200 yards to a half mile, before turning back in a sunwise direction.

Each run out should be longer than the last, for how far she ultimately gets determines how long she will live. The activity makes her brave, seals in an energetic and industrious character, and increases her chances to acquire sheep, horses and children. To shorten her course, or rest, suggests laziness and invites misfortune. Rex told me that he had attended many *Kinaalda*, and joined the crowds running alongside the girl each morning. He was careful never to pass her for fear ''I'd reach old age before her and die first.''

Of the songs given the girl a number encouraged this running. One contains the refrain: ''The breeze coming from her as she runs is beautiful.'' Here is the complete text of a running song from the

First Puberty Ceremony as included in the Navajo Emergence Myth and preserved in the Wheelwright Museum archives in Santa Fe, New Mexico.

My little one, they run out shouting, they run out shouting,
My little one, they run out shouting.
My little one, they run out shouting, they run out shouting,
My little one, they run out shouting.

The White Shell Girl, —they run out shouting—
From below the East, —they run out shouting—
Before her, the wind blows the trees, —they run out shouting—
Behind her, the wind blows the plants, —they run out shouting—
The white shell stands erect all about her, —they run out shouting—
The sacred words, your girl, —they run out shouting—
Before her, all is beautiful, —they run out shouting—
Behind her, all is beautiful, —they run out shouting—

My little one, they run out shouting, they run out shouting,
My little one, they run out shouting.

The Turquoise Girl, —they run out shouting—
From below the West, —they run out shouting—
Behind her, the wind blows the plants, —they run out shouting—
Before her, the wind blows the trees, —they run out shouting—

The turquoise stands erect all about her, —they run out shouting—
The sacred words, your girl, —they run out shouting—
Behind her, all is beautiful, —they run out shouting—
Before her, all is beautiful, —they run out shouting—

My little one, they run out shouting, they run out shouting,
My little one, they run out shouting.
My little one, they run out shouting, they run out shouting,
My little one, they run out shouting.

Among the Apache a girl's puberty was celebrated by the well-known Devil Dance, where masked "Mountain Spirits" with latticework crowns danced around bonfires. Here the girl who ran each day to "make her nature" was remolding herself into the female ideal, White Painted Woman.

Navajo girl running in puberty ritual

Featured in what anthropologists call the "work complex" segment of rite-of-passage ritualism, puberty running was also performed outside the southwest, in the Great Basin, the Plateau, California, up the Pacific Coast, and even in ancient Peru. Perhaps, they conjecture, the trait emerged out of the Northwest Coast, and was disseminated by distant forebears of the Navajo into California and beyond.

Among the Washo the girl carried a decorated six-foot elderberry wand as she ran four times up a hill at night to light four fires. At dawn a male relative finally planted the stick far back in the hills. So long as it remained unbroken, she would be straight-backed and agile. Upon reaching womanhood, Maidu girls would run at top speed at sunrise during their ten-day ceremony. When Karok girls of northern California ran back and forth at dawn, they made motions to the morning star as if to catch it, praying for long life. In the 1890s a southern California Luiseño woman named Yèla Wassuk recalled her people's puberty rite, the *we'enic*. A four-day affair, it culminated in a race to some revered boulders—still found near Rincon and La Jolla—where girls painted red diamonds representing rattlesnakes and deposited braided-hair bracelets and anklets as offerings. During these runs they gave their spirits to Wuyoot, the moon whose symbol was also painted on rocks.

Some California Indian boys ran at puberty too. After rubbing themselves with a poultice of bumble bee comb for power, Pomo lads raced through the hills playing a native form of jews harp; on the ritual's second morning older men would run naked on an eight-mile course. For Serrano youth the ceremony's third day involved a race where the victor became lead dancer in the "whirling" or Eagle Dance. This involved ingesting the sacred *toloache* or jimson weed which the Mountain Cahuilla called the "grass that could talk." Among the Luiseño not far away their *toloache* rite culminated with a footrace whose winners were deemed the tribe's most promising young men. In the southern Sierra Nevada boys and girls joined in a ritual run unrelated to puberty but associated with this jimson weed rite. Practically the entire village joined in, covering the 200 yard circuit around the village many times. They were escorting the "giver" of the drug, some say to hasten its hallucinatory effects.

Both the Achomawi and Yuma included races in their nose-piercing rite for boys about the age of eight or nine. Once the septum was punctured, they were taken on a northerly run of up to fifteen miles. For the next three days this was repeated to the west, the south, and finally the east, as if to integrate them, at this vulnerable moment, with the geography which would nourish them all their lives.

An elaborate boy's puberty festival occurred in Peru. Called the *Waracikoy*, its preparations and sacrifices began in October and were followed by a pilgrimage in November after the fourteen-year-old Incan boys had been "knighted." Their destination was a hill, named Anahuarque, about eight miles from the Incan capital of Cuzco.

The runners first paid homage to a shrine dedicated to a *huaca*, a godlike figure who, it was said, had run like a lion during the Great Flood. At the bottom of the hill waited girls and vessels brimming with maize beer. Down the steep slope, the boys ran and tumbled for 2,000 feet. Some passed out, others died from the ordeal. The survivors were given refreshing beer, and the victor was honored.

The Incan races appear to be a decisive demonstration of physical training. For other tribes running was also an avenue of metaphysical development. Among the Yurok of northern California a refined mode of running involved the fast-action meditation one associates with far eastern mysticism. Early in his work with Yurok elders in the 1970s, it became clear to anthropologist Thomas Buckley that when these people referred to "running" they were thinking about more than the running which was once part of every young man's physical training, along with wrestling, hefting river rocks, and arduous swims.

Buckley had heard of one young man who grew famously strong by running from Terwer Creek up 3,000 feet to the summit of Red Mountain. At first he carried only little rocks with him, but gradually he increased their size until by his mid-twenties he was packing up small boulders, adding to his cairn which remains there today.

Fathers might roll their boys out of bed at dawn to run, particularly on beaches where the sand made or hard pushing. Or on stormy nights they would make them drag heavy redwood dugout canoes up the shore at a clip as training for the "stick game," a Yurok form of shinny.

At this point, however, sons of the most influential families might enter a more rarefied sort of esoteric training. Here running joined a selection of techniques—collectively called *hohkep* ("training")—which enabled young men, and some women, to advance into greater interaction with the unseen forces in the world, in order to accumulate knowledge and control.

According to Buckley, "True running, as far as I can gather, was looked upon as a kind of effortless gliding, what my teacher called 'skimming.' They say runners reaching this state of consciousness could skim over the tops of close-growing manzanita bushes on the southern slopes of the Siskiyou Mountains."

When traditional Yurok culture was in flower, it was common knowledge that such study was perilous. "Power" can be diverted to either benign or malevolent intent; true running could become a sorcerer's weapon as well as a means towards positive spiritual growth. Buckley emphasizes it is misleading to accept the tie between trance-running and sorcery as stressed in contemporary oral history on Yurok running without appreciating that once it was equally vital for extending a Yurok student's benevolent membership in the natural flow of the world's "pure" energies.

The aspiring runner, Buckley explains, was taught to "establish an extrasensory relationship with the trail, through singing to it, addressing it. He was taught to make room for it, to receive the trail as a being, letting it dictate the run. It was as though the trail was running out behind him and under him by itself. This might be practised at first by running hard along a trail with eyes closed, trusting the trail itself to guide you." As one's abilities developed, riskier types of altered-state running might be learned.

Another technique was visualization, to help the student "learn to feel that the actual energies being used are the world's rather than one's own. Rather than feeling how your feet hit the ground, emphasis is placed on feeling the ground pushing back up against your feet. Gradually you put more and more trust in the earth, and move into a light trance state when you're no longer interfering in the running. Here the running is just happening; whether the world is doing it or you are doing it is of no importance.'' The trainee was taught how to ''see'' the air rushing by as a sort of rope along which he could pull himself through breathing techniques and hand motions.

The control derived through such practices was sometimes invested in a talisman, known as ''a foot.'' Personally acquired through training, but also loaned or even purchased, it enabled people to cover long distances at fantastic speeds. Buckley heard of a man, who owned such a ''foot,'' racing a horse from the Klamath River to San Rafael, almost 250 miles to the south, arriving in plenty of time to wait for the rider to gallop in.

A ''foot'' might be used by sorcerers to go ''deviling'' at night over long stretches. ''The old time sorcerers, the *uma'a* in Yurok language, were great runners,'' says Buckley. ''And they're deceptive. They could send out their 'shadows'—five subtle bodies—running down the trail ahead of them. If you want to catch a sorcerer—and you do because they'll make you rich—you let the five shadow-bodies go running past, but grab the sixth. That's the real *uma'a*.''

In one tale of sorcerer-running collected by Buckley, a dedicated runner was practising hard at night when a woman came running directly at him. To one side of the trail was a six-foot embankment with a fence above it. Suddenly, the woman shot into the air, straight over bank and fence. He recognized her, and teased her later about being a ''devil.'' She had not only disclosed her sorcerer's running ability, but also the leaping power associated with another Yurok ''medicine,'' that of a ''big heart,'' a fighting specialist.

While running power figures heavily in such sorcery accounts, it was also central to the positive, ''high medicine'' practices undertaken in sacred mountain precincts far from the river villages. Buckley's mentor told him about his own ''graduation exercise'' from his esoteric training. For three days he ran into the mountains, covering some twenty miles as the crow flies, finally reaching his special rock.

''These are the roughest mountains, up and down canyons, so

perhaps it was a hundred miles all told. He ran this in three stages, at night only, by the dark of the moon, resting and meditating during the days. His own teacher hung back, about a half-day behind, to catch up if there was trouble. At one point in his run a grizzly bear walked into his path up ahead. He described the feeling of being able to run straight through the grizzly if it didn't get out of the way. He said he charged it at full speed, and the bear shrieked in fear and crashed into the bush.''

At mid-afternoon the Hopis pass through the stone portals of the College of Ganado, its grounds as green as an oasis. They are some forty-five miles from their final destination and still in the thick of Navajo country, but this school's mandate is to serve both tribes. I notice on the school's bulletin board that a 5,000 meter ''Navahopi Trail Race'' for women has been scheduled this very afternoon, but I suspect few Hopis will be interested or available.

Plans for the Hopi crew to stay over in the vacant dorms have gone awry. The boys flop on the soft lawns, fire frisbees at each other, and get photographed while their coordinators locate quarters. Meanwhile, decorated pickups and cars, parked grill to trunk, crowd the area. The mystery is explained: from a central building exits a Navajo wedding party, groom in powder-blue tux, his bride in her showroom gown. Once the rice and slamming of car door rituals are over, the procession snakes around the campus. The Hopis are feeling devilish and respond like maniacs. The Navajos are trapped in their cars as a pile of wild-eyed boys in what looks like Dayglo underwear descend upon them, howling each time a pretty bridesmaid's car slinks by.

Tonight matters are more serious. From Hopi country arrives the tribal chairman and a *Wuwuchim* priest to hold a retreat for the runners at the nearby lake. Among the items reportedly discussed is the ritual disposal of the corn and prayer plume. Since San Juan and Zia, I learn later, these offerings changed the nature of the run, moving it more into the context of classic Hopi ritual. For this the boys were unprepared, and the responsibility has changed them too. That is what Bruce Talawema was trying to tell me three days ago. Although we have been the only outsiders to stick with them the entire way, we are not welcome at the retreat. We are uninitiated, and this Hopi homecoming, like that of the Zuni, is really for members only.

Group portrait at Ganado, 9 August 1980

Hair-cutter Runner Kachina

7.

Ganado to Hopi Cultural Center
10 August

THE FINAL STRETCH
WHEN RUNNERS BECOME CLOUDS: SNAKE DANCE RACE
HOPI MIDNIGHT RUNS, CLAN RACES, AND RUNNER KACHINAS
NATION OF RUNNERS: THE TARAHUMARA STORY
CLIMAX OF THE TRICENTENNIAL RUN:
THE ALL-PUEBLO RENEWAL

THE GERMAN TOURIST came for Indians and now they are engulfing her. Last night her tour bus climbed 600 feet up Second Mesa, passed the turnoff to Shungopavi, "place of the sand-grass spring," oldest and most conservative of the thirteen Hopi villages, and stopped four miles later at this thirty-three unit museum/motel complex. The highway is crowded with Hopis drawn here by village criers this morning. Jamming the rooftops of the Pueblo-style tourist facility, teenagers are chattering and eyeing the road for any signs of runners. Antsy crowds are crushing the flimsy tables displaying arts and crafts in front of the museum. In the picnic grounds women stir corn, stew and coffee in ten-gallon tubs for a runner's potluck.

"Their adrenals are up," Mike Kabotie teases me. An artist like his father Fred, he is on the Run's planning committee. "They might string you up," he grins. It is a reminder of what this celebration is really about. The German tourist takes refuge beside me in the museum's portal.

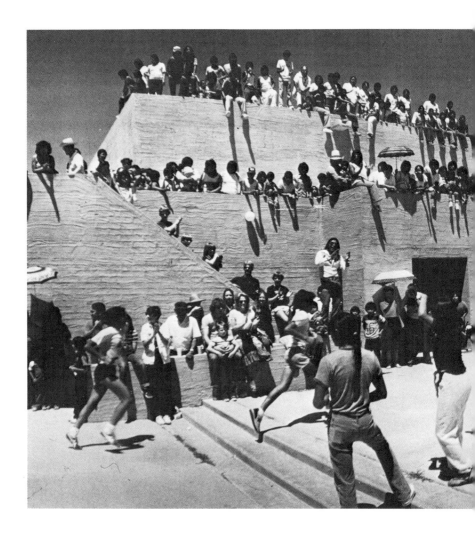

Last night at Ganado it was agreed that all the Pueblo runners, eastern and western, could run into the center en masse. The reception committee would feature Abbott Sekaquaptewa, the craggy, handsome Hopi Tribal Chairman whose movements on aluminum crutches are oddly charismatic, and famed Hopi painter, Fred Kabotie, eighty years old this year.

Looking somewhat lost Kabotie himself wanders by to ask at the Museum desk where exactly he is to greet them. A little, erect man,

Runners entering Hopi Cultural Center, 10 August 1980

wearing glasses, there is an understated elegance about him. In 1959 this complex was a gleam in his eye. First he had a fight to bring water lines up Second Mesa, at odds with both older traditionalists among his people and a recalcitrant U. S. government. The Hopi silverwork and carving guilds were his ideas. At last the Museum was built with a motel and restaurant, a neutral center for all the independent and sometimes quarreling Hopi towns. This morning Hopi waitresses in versions of traditional navy blue dresses with single shoulder straps served us blue corn grits, *nokquivi*, (hominy stew), *piki* or fried bread.

These tourist depots serve a cunning function for Indian communities concerned about cultural privacy. It might not have been a conscious item in their planning, but they provide buffer zones for absorbing, directing or deflecting the insistent curiosity of outsiders. They apportion degrees of cultural goods and information, from native-made and signed crafts for sale to the casual tourist, to books and tips for the aficionados who want to attend a specific ceremony. As checkpoints between cultural worlds, they help to put access back under Indian control.

Since the late nineteenth century Hopiland has drawn the cultivated pilgrim; the tribe's well-publicized philosophy and ritual life have made it the Athens of the Indian world. This morning the motel is booked solid for the next three weeks because Third Mesa is about to hold its Snake-Antelope Festival, ever a drawing-card for non-Indians. During the hippie heyday a new stream of seekers saw these mesas as America's Nepal. Whatever the wave of the moment, the Cultural Center helps the tribe keep tabs on who's around. Shortly after visitors arrive they are taken over by the Hopi ambience; the Center imposes an appropriate pace and etiquette without actually telling you how to behave.

This morning the runners left Ganado in the dark. Running two-mile laps so everyone might get their fill, they reached the sandy battlements of Steamboat Canyon by about 9:30. Seven more miles carried them into their 631,174-acre homeland enclosing three slender mesas jutting like battleships into the Painted Desert. Perched along their crests are eleven of the Hopi villages, pointed toward the San Francisco Peaks a hundred miles to the southwest, abode of their rain-bringing kachinas.

Another twenty miles takes the runners to Keams Canyon, where most of their parents attended Bureau of Indian Affairs boarding school. By noon the caravan of cars behind them weaves for a mile and grows each minute. Next they reach the recent Hopi settlement of Polacca on the yucca and sagebrush desert below First Mesa, not far from where Hopis once enshrined the heart of a Navajo chief slain in battle. A tourist guide warns, "Side roads and footpaths may be considered sacred or of ritual importance." This countryside is alive with pilgrimage routes and shrines; you hunt for a cactus to take home and come upon scraggly bushes fluttering with eagle down and pine needle prayer sticks.

Yet the Hopis are not exempt from modern anxieties. "I wish I could speak to you of the green valleys here with flowers blooming, where the children are playing and the grandmothers are making piki bread," Wayne Sekaquaptewa told a *New York Times* reporter, "but that is not what is happening here." As publisher of the Hopi newspaper, *Qua'Toqati*, Sekaquaptewa is close to the contradictions between two ways of everyday life. "You can talk to the wisest man out here, a man who can tell you all there is to know about the clouds and plants and the animals, and what use is that to you when you have to be at your nine-to-five job in twenty minutes?"

Camouflaged and flush above the prow of the First Mesa lies Walpi, not an inch of wasted space. Three miles further and the runners are near the earlier site of Shungopavi, before it was rebuilt on top of Second Mesa following the rebellion. Here San Bartholomew Church once stood, built of hewn pine timbers which the Franciscans forced Hopis to drag from the San Francisco peaks. When the people ambushed Father Joseph de Trujillo 300 years ago today, first they hung him from one of those pine vigas, then burned him and used the timbers for their kiva roofs. They also threw church records and saints' effigies into the fire. When they suspected fellow Hopi at the Pueblo of Awatovi of warming to Catholic missionaries, they trapped its people in their own kivas and burned them to death.

In 1976, when Fred Kabotie was invited to contribute to the Bicentennial Show at the Museum of Santa Fe, he departed from his customary scenes of Hopi dances and gentle village life. He painted Father Trujillo with a broken neck swaying from a torn beam. Behind him San Bartholomew is being dismantled, and a fire is being kindled with an old-style bow drill. "That was my Bicentennial painting," Kabotie said. The Hopi memory is long, but today has allowed for a happier recollection of their revolution.

Runner Kachina masks.

Traditionally, running is interwoven into the entire Hopi year. In 1921 a Hopi named Crow Wing from the First Mesa village of Sichumovi kept a remarkable diary. Hardly a month passed, from February through December, without its appropriate running event. Among the most hallowed were the races held at dawn on the nineteenth morning of the Snake-Antelope ceremony. Runners start from a spring in the desert and bring symbolic rainfall to their kivas. Fred Kabotie recalls when he stood with his friends below Shungopavi mesa, waiting to join the Snake runners for their last stretch.

That year, 1906, was tense. His people were divided over the government's campaign to ban tribal rituals and the accompanying sacred races. More urgently, Kabotie's traditionalist grandparents were under attack by reservation officials for not sending their children to school to learn white ways. Young Fred ran three miles back and forth to Toreva Day School each day, and suffered the indignity of having his long hair hacked off.

This was the age when he began the running exercise program expected of every Hopi boy. But the Snake-Antelope races were something special. Shungopavi criers alerted everyone early that morning. Five miles from the mesa, the race starter told chosen runners to speed like antelopes. "The priest put this mud on their feet, bluish color, from the bottom of the sacred spring," said Kabotie. As the sun appeared the priest smashed one water-filled gourd and prayed that rain would so drench their fields. "By that time the priest had made circles on the ground ahead of the runners, and the lead fellow who carries the sacred spring water in his gourd was running, running." Holding corn stalks and melon and squash vines, Fred and his friends watched the runners draw near, handing ahead the netted gourd at each pass so it remained in front. "We joined in at

This photo sequence (pages 155-157) shows the Snake-Antelope Dance runners of the Hopi. First, the ritual runners are spotted approaching the mesa (page 155, top). As they begin to scramble up the sheer side of the mesa, they keep passing the gourd of sacred water ahead to the front runner (page 155, bottom).

The lead man races for his kiva (page 156, top), while youngsters holding corn and squash vines greet them (page 156, bottom). The winning racer in 1901 at the village of Mishongnovi, a man named Talahkuiwa, posed beside his kiva (page 157).

157

the base of the mesa, and all of us headed for the plaza. We were doing it because we were the clouds. The people were the clouds, do you see? We were the clouds coming to give us rain."

Seventy-four years later, the Snake dance of 1980 revealed little change. "We drove around my friend's field below Hotevilla and through the wash," Hopi scholar Robert Black told me afterward, "I think it was near Sun Spring, where the water and mud had been gathered. There must have been about twelve racers when we got there. There were pickups and cars. It was just before dawn, and cool. The two Snake priests were standing about 100 yards apart, barefoot, their bodies painted black, wearing Snake kilts, their long hair hanging down free and eagle feathers blowing in the breeze.

"Between them stood the lone Antelope priest, holding the small gourd. The runners lined up facing east. Suddenly the Antelope Priest, about fifty years old, took off towards Hotevilla." He also carried a little wheel fashioned of reeds, symbolic of the four directions, a prayer that "dry washes may rush and flood their thirsty fields."

"The Snake priests began running at each other," Black went on, "back and forth in front of the runners four times. The last time the boys took off. We went ahead to Hotevilla. At the mesa I noticed others waiting for them, their arms full of the products of their fields. Everyone followed the front runner with the gourd scrambling up the footpath.

"At the top, the aunts of the men began a mock battle with them over the vegetables, the men holding them out of reach. There was great commotion, a lot of joviality and excitement. Meanwhile the lead runner entered his kiva where the priest blessed him and the water. Then he was privileged to take the water for his own fields." Of the tussle on the mesa top, Crow Wing wrote, "The meaning of it is to hurry the watermelon and the corn to ripen . . . When it rains and there is lots of water, the animals will be happy and run around . . . If a girl gets lots of melons and corn, and baskets and pottery, her father will have lots of crops in the fall."

Running and fertility are so entwined in Hopi consciousness that the one action generally implies the other. At group prayers for rain and growth like the Snake and Basket dances, or in solitary moments when a farmer communes with his sandy corn patch, running is an important medium. One planting ritual calls for a brave man to impersonate the deity of fire and the original owner of Hopi lands, the dread Masau. It is a hazardous role. During his four-day seclusion he must sleep in a darkened room, eat no salt or meat, only corn ''so as to become skinny and a fast runner.'' At midnight he comes out to run in successively tightening circuits, counter-clockwise, corralling the clouds almost as if they were wild horses. He ends up in a final run around the base of his own mesa. It is reputedly a fearful experience. ''It is dangerous to go out at night like this,'' anthropologist Ernest Beaglehole was told. ''One man, just initiated, went out on the first night. He became so crazy with fear that he tried to kill himself by throwing himself over the mesa edge onto the rocks below . . . When a man runs at night and sees something moving in front of him, he must go up to the thing whether it turns out to be bush, tree or stone, and rub some of the stuff of which the thing is made over his body. This will make him brave and no longer afraid.''

By the Snake-Antelope races of mid-summer, the running season was well under way. Hopi kick-ball games would have been going on since February; at Oraibi the season opened shortly after the Kachina cult initiation known as *Powamu*. The balls were made of sandstone, piñon sap, or micaceous materials which have been powdered, mixed with urine and formed into nodules. Sometimes sap balls were laced with horse hair from fast steeds; at Oraibi the big toe hairs of noted runners added power.

Called *wunpa-namunwa*, Hopi kick-ball generally followed the Papago pattern except the Hopi circuits took them around springs below their mesas. The games were sometimes said to shield fields within their perimeter from sandstorms; the balls themselves were often laid on Powamu altars. Once, it was said, young men practised all year for kick-ball; one awoke before dawn to the sound of the runners' bells as they ran to cast cornmeal at the springs. Opposing kiva teams kicked the balls for a distance of four miles through soft sand before getting home, with the winners booting theirs over the mesa's edge. As race season progressed, runs could cover eight to ten miles. Players wrapped their big toes with cotton, but even so often returned home with swollen insteps.

Until planting time, competitive racing was declared open. Betting was allowed, and races took on more gusto. Social life hummed with kivas and clans playing kick-ball, "zig-zag" races, and twenty-five-mile distance runs against each other. Runners wore identifying feathers, garments or body paint with such clan markings as bluebird, sun, moon and antelope. In mid-February, 1934, anthropologist Mischa Titiev painted a white clay star on his chest, a crescent moon on his back, and joined in.

"One approached the ball as soon as it landed," he later wrote, "and propelled it forward again, while the others ran on ahead once more. In spite of the pauses for 'kicking' the race went at a far faster pace than I had anticipated . . . It was remarkable to see how the runners, barefooted though they were, plunged into cactus or thorny bushes without the slightest hesitation." As they closed in on Old Oraibi, Titiev was impressed by the front-runner. "It was some stunt for a kid of about nine to have run barefooted about three and one-half miles and to have finished in the lead, despite a mile-long steep upgrade at the finish."

In Hopi folklore the Antelope and Chicken Hawk race ends with the creation of a runner's shrine containing Chicken Hawk's heart, a three-sided cell with a stone slab seal. "If anyone wishes to be strong

Kick-ball race circuit below
Walpi on first mesa, 1889

160

in running," Chicken Hawk advised, "he shall pray there and I will give him strength."

Accompanying his father on a salt pilgimage, Don Talayesva was "in the Zuni forests," when the two stopped, and raced to this shrine, playing tortoise and hare. "We raced up a mesa with the (cornmeal) dough and placed it with prayer feathers in a small hole for the Hawk deity. As we moved down the southern slope, my father said, 'There is a long slab of stone; jump upon it and spring to the opposite side.' As we completed the jump he said, 'Well, we have performed the rites correctly, and our reward will be rain.' " So the Hopis address the Hawk in their running song:

> *Be racing.*
> *With joyful words*
> *Be racing.*
> *The abdomen, the back.*
> *Hawk*
> *Be racing.*

The most entertaining Hopi running event occurred in early spring, around planting time, with the appearance of the *Wawash katchinum*, the runner-kachinas. The Hopi boast the greatest array of these "overtaking" kachinas, at least twenty masked figures, each dubbed for the punishment inflicted on men they can catch. In 1979 Fred Kabotie got hilariously caught up in their antics.

"At this time, in April, these special kachinas come to the village just to make the people run. First they get all fixed up down in the kiva, then go off to the edge of the mesa before going from kiva to kiva, saying, 'We are contesting you in running. Everybody come.' So they challenge you, and when one catches you, the *Choquapolo*, that Mud Kachina, he hits your back or anywhere with mud. *Hemsona*, or Hair-Cutter Kachina, he clips off your hair if he gets you. *Tsil* Kachina puts hot chili in your mouth. *Kokopell'Mana*, they knock down their victims and pretend copulation on them. That's where the fun comes in. Those two *Kokopell* caught me, and there was a big fight when my aunts rushed in to pull me loose."

Other characters tear off their victims' clothes, stick burrs into their hair, push dog manure into their mouths, rub fat and soot into their faces, slap them with rabbit-hunting sticks or yucca whips. Their seasonal entrance suggests heightened interaction between men, crops, earth and rainclouds. But these mischief-makers can go too far, as suggested in a tale recorded by Edward S. Curtis at Walpi. Furious when the Hair-Cutter Kachina cut his son's locks, an early chief turned his twelve-year-old daughter into a champion runner and disguised her in a Hair-Cutter Kachina mask. She whipped all the best runners, sliced off their hair, and escaped. When word leaked that the men had been humiliated by a girl, a long-distance grudge run was scheduled. The winning faction would behead the losers. The race turned out to be more a contest among spirit helpers, Chicken Hawk for the girl, Dove for the fastest men. Hawk plucked out Dove's feathers, enabling her to streak home first. Both sides decided that instead of slaughtering an entire section of the village, the runners themselves should die. The fastest male runner was beheaded, the girl buried alive near a spring. Both factions abandoned the community and migrated in separate directions, as if the ground were forever violated.

Such stories and customs perplex the outsider. In his

Runner Kachinas on first mesa, c. 1905.

autobiography, edited by Leo Simmons, Don Talayesva recalled an episode in which a *Kokopell 'Mana* Kachina challenged him. He outran her and initiated a mock copulation. The audience enjoyed themselves greatly, but Don noticed the local school principal scowling in disgust. He cut the demonstration short. When the kachina was released she received prayer sticks for the cloud people and told the runners, "All right, your reward shall be rain."

Talayesva walked over to the principal. "Well, white man," he said, "you want to see what goes on, don't you? You have spoiled our prayers, and it may not rain. You think this business is vulgar, but it means something sacred to us. This old kachina is impersonating the Corn Maiden; therefore we must have intercourse with her so that our corn will increase and our people will live in plenty. If this were evil we would not be doing it. You are supposed to be an educated man, but you had better go back to school and learn something more about Hopi life."

Below the Mexican border another Indian nation places less emphasis on running as collective ritual than they do on its importance to transportation, social cohesion, and a good time. No indigenous people in the world have their work, play and identity revolve so intimately around running as that of the Tarahumara whose name for themselves, *Raamuri*, derives from their principal running game. Up and down the waves of twenty or more steep barrancas in the Sierra de Tarahumara in southwestern Chihuahua, these fiercely independent, shy people move on foot day and night. About 40,000 strong, they are spread throughout scattered ranchos and caves in the 35,000-square-mile wilderness. The dramatic variations in terrain require them to farm corn and herd goats between coniferous forests at 9000 feet and tropical canyon bottoms with bamboo and orange groves—where they winter. Daily life sees them on the run from childhood; men over sixty herd at top speed. They are superb porters and mail-carriers, they run down deer, and they play their form of kick-ball—known as *ralajipame*—at every opportunity, from pickup games during drinking parties to multi-day events where villages compete against one another.

Karl Kernberger has travelled to the Tarahumara country six times since 1957, and photographed their running events. "I remember one especially," he told me. "It lasted a couple days and when they ran at night they carried torches. It seemed the runners had boundless energy. I don't recall injuries, and nobody ever seemed tired. They were concentrating as they kicked that ball of madrone wood on and on. They didn't seem to be pushing themselves or crossing any pain threshold. They just seemed to be doing what the Tarahumara have to do, run."

Tarahumara women playing Hoop Race, 1971

Kernberger is but among the most recent Tarahumara visitors to comment on their stamina and speed. In the 1880s Frederick Schwatka described them running with forty pounds of mail and provisions on their backs from Botapilas to Chihuahua City—500 miles of unpaved roads. Still they stopped over for the night in Chihuahua City so as not to miss the bullfight.

In 1894 Carl Lumholz describes Tarahumaras running "easily 170 miles without stopping," and describes Mexicans hiring them to collect wild horses. "It may take two or three days, but they will bring them in, the horses, thoroughly exhausted, while the men who, of course, economize their strength, are comparatively fresh . . . they will run down a deer, following it for days through snow and rain, until the animal is cornered and easily shot with arrows or, until it is overtaken utterly jaded and its hoofs dropping off.''

Around 1900 Alexander S. Shepherd hired Tarahumara *cargadores* to haul an upright piano through 185 mountainous miles. Spelling each other every half-hour, three sets of men made the trip in little over fifteen days. Then they sprinted the same distance home in three days.

In 1924 Ernest Thompson Seton describes a Tarahumara postman who routinely covered 70 miles a day, seven days a week, bearing a heavy mailbag.

In 1929 John A. White gave further details of these mail couriers. ''He is always on an easy run that must carry him along six or seven miles an hour at least . . . the carrier does not run the whole length of these windings in descending a hill. He cuts off the corners at each bend by placing his hand on the edge of the trail, and vaulting to the lower level whenever the two are not more than six or eight feet apart. All this time he never gives up the dog trot that is carrying him so rapidly and surely. . . . One day a party which had reached the Cumbre (mountain crest) sent a Tarahumara courier with a letter to the mine (6,000 feet into the Barranca del Cobre) and this swift-footed son of the Sierra made the trip to the bottom, and returned with an answer in an hour and a half, running the entire distance up and down.''

In 1935 anthropologists Wendell C. Bennett and Robert M. Zingg describe Tarahumaras regularly hired as messengers and food porters at a mere twenty-five centavos a day. They went faster than mules, started earlier in the morning, and covered at least twice the distance with over fifty-pound loads which they balanced on their shoulders or strapped to their backs.

In 1963 a group of American river-runners ran low on food and had to climb out of the Barranca del Cobre. Some Tarahumara chanced by and helped them out. ''At one point,'' wrote one of the

166

Americans, "as we toiled upwards, the Indians passed us each carrying a sixty-pound pack of our gear. Suddenly I realized it was their third trip of the day."

In 1971 on one of his many trips to Tarahumara country, film-maker William E. Sagstetter encountered a Tarahumara carrying his crippled wife on his back for sixty miles. Later, while he was visiting the Indians at El Divisdero, a Tarahumara made a twenty-four mile trip to get Sagstetter pipe tobacco.

In 1971 Michael Jenkinson was told about a Tarahumara courier who left the Sisoguichie Jesuit mission to check on health conditions in his people's villages, and covered fifty miles in six hours including stops en route.

In 1976 James Norman exhausted himself descending 4,000 feet into one Tarahumara canyon, only to be passed by two loping Indians shouldering ten-foot wooden beams for houses which they had cut and were delivering green for eight cents each.

In 1979 Bernard L. Fontana bought a sixty-five pound earthen-ware jar for the Arizona State Museum and hired an elderly Tarahumara to carry it out of the canyon. The old man made the sixteen-mile trip that night and was back by dawn.

As early as the 17th century, Spanish chroniclers were aware of the Tarahumara's "fondness for games." By then their national sport had switched from the pre-Columbian rubber ball game to kick-ball. Today their teams rove over low, level ridges either around a cross-country route or back and forth between boundaries marked by crosses cut into trees. Whether these *vueltas* are linear or circular they cover them many times, some races totalling forty miles. Before each event it is customary to line up as many rocks as there are *vueltas*; as one is completed a rock is removed. The sport is as important to the audience as it is to the runners. This is also true for popular women's races, where a hoop replaces the ball. In their bright shawls and flowing skirts the women use wooden forks to pass the hoops ahead. During kick-ball, the spectators stand on higher ground to take in the show and sometimes run alongside them. Below, the players splash through streams, scoot along fences,

The world of Tarahumara running, in photos from the 1930s to the 1970s. Balls for their kick-racing are carved from hard wood (page 168, top). Before the races the betting requires careful equalizing of the stakes (page 168, bottom). During the daytime the racers bound through mountain streams (page 169, top) and trot over rock-strewn ridges (page 169, bottom). Instead of stopping at nightfall, they continue their running by the light of the pitch-pine torches (page 170).

shovel their calloused feet into spiny cacti for caught balls, come and go around the crags and hollows. At night they flash through the canyons by the light of pitch-pine torches.

Refereeing the races are *chokeame*, respected elders who travel amongst the far-flung ranchos to issue challenges. Because of the heavy betting these events must be negotiated with utmost care and confidentiality. Once the location, date and number of runners is established, the men themselves are picked, and a three-day preparation period begins. Training is hardly a factor, since daily life keeps everybody stretched and trim. However there are pre-race rituals and dietary restrictions. If the race is associated with a *teseguinado*, the frequent drinking parties where Tarahumara social interaction is intensified with the help of warm maize beer, the runners restrict themselves to cedar tea. Along with cedar smoke, the tea will be used to ''cure'' their legs for the match. From strangers they take no corn *pinole*, the common food, or water. They avoid fats, potatoes, and eggs.

Magic-making is not as prevalent today, but the *jumame*, runners, are still quarantined prior to the race. Copal incense is burned for them and songs tell of Grey Fox, the runner of Tarahumara folklore. On race day ''remedies'' are brought by runners and their friends. Their footmen of old wore woven charm belts festooned with deer hooves, sections of reed, pebble rattles and cartridge shells said to keep them awake on longer runs. A glowworm might be concealed in their cotton loincloth, and they tied on Macaw or peacock feathers, birds considered ''light-footed and mysterious.'' Their faces and legs were spotted with white earth. These days their apparel includes Mexican straw hats and pants, which are usually shed as the running progresses until they wear only shorts or loincloths with but one sandal to leave the kicking foot bare.

In the haggling over stakes nothing is exempt, bows, bars of soap, clothing, sheep, goats, cattle, even land, sometimes amounting to thousand-peso bets. With such high stakes races are sometimes thrown, runners accepting bribes to let the other side get ahead. Generally the *chokeame* keep the games fair, and discourage such fouls as runners tripping each other up, tearing off each other's loincloths, or handling the ball.

At the outset the runners, up to forty in some events, might bunch together. Some seem merely plodding, but they can turn out to be crucial toward the finish. Others perform as helpers for long-distance experts and the finalists who pour it on in the last laps. Hour after hour, mile after mile they run. Along their way fans strive within and outside the rules to help, rubbing down their men, feeding them finely-ground parched corn mixed with water for quick energy. At these two-mile rest stops shamans are available to revive tired or hurting runners with *sinonowa* root mixed with fat for hurting joints, *bakanori* root to counteract evil in the legs, or *kotcinawa* herb to burn and blow towards the opposition to make them sleepy.

To energize themselves in the past, runners chewed the green tops of *jikuri* and *peyote cimarron* cacti or drank them in boiled solution. (Accounts suggest that this activated the plants' stimulating, not hallucinatory, ingredients; running visions are not recorded for the Tarahumara.)

Toward the finish an entire crowd runs alongside for encouragement. The team behind might drop out, but for an official win runners must go the distance. "One notable feature at the end of a race," writes Michael Kennedy, a leading student of Tarahumara culture, "is the lack of attention paid the winning runner. He is left alone after his great physical effort while everyone concentrates upon collecting his winnings. There is no back-slapping or hurrahs. His winning seems taken for granted, although spectators who have won large amounts are later expected to pay a token of appreciation to the winning runners."

To Kennedy, "Racing is more than a game to the Tarahumara. Though obviously a pleasant diversion, it is also an economic activity, a force for social cohesion, and a channel for aggression. . .if this institution were removed from Tarahumara life, the total cultural imbalance resulting would be greater than if some sporting activity were dropped from our own complex culture. . . ."

A roar from the crowd. The German tourist has gathered her courage to ask me what's going on just as sirens open up. A wall of runners swerves like a herd from the highway toward us. We are crammed against the cool stucco walls.

Leading the throng is a Hopi in damp yellow T-shirt, gripping the eagle plume *paho* from Zia and the pouch. Beside him a boy holds fast to the ear of blue corn. By the German tourist's watch it is 12:15. A line of seven clan mothers stands ready. Kabotie holds the corn high and prays, then hands it to the lead clan mother. He unrolls the message and his voice cracks as he reads it aloud; he holds it aloft for all to see. The pouch, message and knotted thong will be buried in a "time capsule" in the unfinished rock shrine directly behind him—a

Taos runners greeted by Hopi elders, 10 August 1980

173

non-Indian idea perhaps fitting for this neutral ground. As for the plume and corn, within the hour they will be the focus of a secluded prayer session. The fluffy prayer stick will be left near a spring as a traditional rain prayer. The corn will be turned over to priests from Shungopavi who officiate the *Soyal*, or Hopi "new year" ceremony. Its kernels will be distributed among them for later planting, as a blessing for the crops of every Hopi.

Herman Agoyo has linked up with the group of eastern Pueblo runners who have made it the entire way. Theatrically he studies his watch for a moment, and then exclaims over the scratchy loudspeaker, "At this moment, 300 years ago, the churches were burning, all the priests had been killed, and the rest of the Spanish were escaping on roads toward Santa Fe." Non-Indians in the crowd stare blankly, every one else gives a cheer.

Wielding the mike like a rock performer, runner Bruce Hamana describes how being Hopi now means something new to the boys who came from Taos all the way home. He chokes back tears and explains how those words in Taos, "This is more than a race. . . . It goes beyond athletics. . . . We're doing this for the people", have become real for them.

Beneath the hot sun old and young now shuffle quietly along an endless reception line. Each runner is blessed: hands shaken lightly and then lifted towards the mouths of their greeters. The runners seem grave and shy at the attention.

Although we have shared something with these young men over the past week, and they have nodded at us warmly today, we feel out of place. The German tourist senses something too and says uncomfortably, "I don't think I should be here."

In a way we have barged in on the first family reunion in 300 years. The runners are still clad in modern track togs, and tomorrow tribal frictions and nine-to-five jobs will resume, but for a moment out of time the beleaguered Pueblo world has been knit together again by fast men on foot bearing the message of their essential separateness, their essential unity.

The run is completed—Fred Kabotie displaying pouch, 10 August 1980

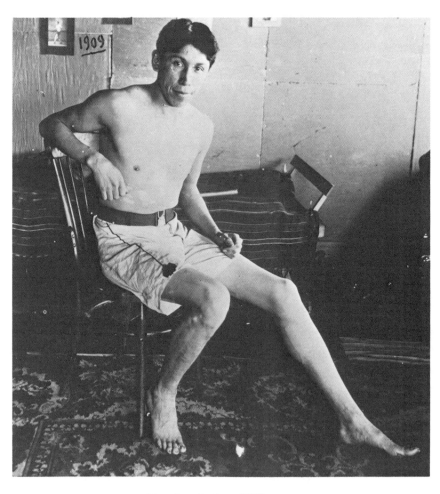

Tom Longboat, c. 1909

8.

In the White Man's Arena

INDIANS RAN their own way.

"White fellows rest before a race," said a Pueblo boy just back from boarding school, "but we stay up all night." Indian runners employed different training techniques, preparation vigils, supernatural helpers, diet, use of emetics and foot care. The forms, meanings and spirit of their traditional running also bore little resemblance to non-Indian running events. They did not translate smoothly to success on the white man's tracks just as whatever the non-Indian might gain from the ways of Indian running must involve more than mimicry.

Since the sixteenth century Indians were imported to Europe to dance, sing, perform arts and crafts and, on occasion, run. The early Seneca runners Deerfoot and Dji′wa′ traveled to compete on the continent. In the eighteenth century a Micmac Indian was shipped to France and put in an amphitheatre with a deer. To demonstrate Indian hunting he stalked and killed the animal, roasted and ate its meat, then, wrote Micmac scholar Silas Rand, "to take a mischievous revenge upon them for making an exhibition of him, he went into a corner of the yard and eased himself before them all."

In the United States the Indian's impact on the sports world arose out of the boarding school system which began in the nineteenth-century as a systematic effort to separate Indian youngsters from their cultural and family ties. In eastern Canada, however, the early marathoner Tom Longboat appeared directly from his Iroquoian roots. He belonged to the Onondaga tribe of the Iroquois Confederacy and was born July 4, 1886 on the Six Nations Reserve. As a boy Longboat practised by chasing cows. When his family picked fruit he ran the twenty-six miles between the orchards near Hamilton and his home reserve. He began racing in local fairs and soon was working out under the guidance of another Six Nations Indian, Bill Davis. In 1909, Davis had finished second in both the Boston Marathon and the American Amateur Athletic Championship Marathon.

Longboat's first major engagement was a ten-miler around Burlington Bay in 1906. He came in first at 49:25; his stride was so disarmingly effortless that officials didn't believe their watches. The unknown Indian later entered the fifteen-mile Ward Marathon in Toronto, a tougher course over bad roads. He won by 500 yards, and was primed for the 1907 Boston Marathon.

The day was unseasonably cold and sleet made conditions worse. Over 200,000 spectators were on hand as Longboat held seventh place for the first ten miles. In the next five he gained on his competitors one by one. For the last ten miles the hills were his. The five-foot, 140 pound Onondaga, against whom the odds were 100 to 1, came in at 2:24:29 4/5, almost five minutes ahead of the previous record. The "Bronze Mercury" continued to star in long distance events, but this was his finest hour.

During his participation in the 1908 Olympic marathon in London he had to drop out from heat exhaustion. Inept handling of his professional career brought trouble, nor was it easy to be an Indian athlete. He moved from job to job, for a time driving a cab in New

York. But loyal service as a soldier in World War I, and his running legacy, won him entry into the Canadian Indian Hall of Fame.

In 1899 the major architect of the United States Government's boarding school policy, a former Indian fighter named Colonel Richard Pratt, hired Glenn Scobie "Pop" Warner to shape up the Carlisle Indian School athletic program in Pennsylvania. Warner was the prototypical hard-driving, intrinsically lovable American coach. Initially, the Indian kids disliked his foul language and gruff commands, but soon his approach mellowed, perhaps as he saw the promise in such football players as Isaac Seneca, Hugh Wheelock and Frank Hudson.

Warner's own career began to ascend with the arrival on campus of a sixteen-year-old boy of mixed Sauk-Fox, Potowatomi and Irish descent named James Francis Thorpe, or Wathohuck—"Bright Path"—in the Fox language. He quickly became the pride of Warner's famous "Indian boys" who excelled in every football and track event Carlisle entered until, in 1912, the best of them qualified to compete in the Olympics in Stockholm.

Another Warner protege, the Hopi Louis Tewanima, had by then made a runner's name for himself. He was sent to Carlisle in 1907 as part of the mandatory schooling program and, according to folklore, assured Warner at the time, "Me run fast good. All Hopi run fast good." Born around 1879 in the same village as Fred Kabotie, Tewanima belonged to the Sand Clan. It was said he would run the 120 miles from home to Winslow and back, barefoot, just to watch the trains pass. At school he once missed the train for a race in Harrisburg and ran the eighteen miles from Carlisle in time to enter and win the two-mile event.

Under Warner, Tewanima joined Longboat in the 1908 London Olympiad, coming in ninth in a field of fifty-six in the marathon. On May 6, 1911, he was one of over a thousand participants in the New York, "half marathon," sponsored by the Evening Mail Newspaper, which ran from 184th Street and Jerome Avenue to City Hall. The young Hopi placed first with a time of 1:09:6.

The following year gave these Carlisle youth their place in sports

Jim Thorpe

Louis Tewanima

history. At the awards presentation for the 1912 Olympic Games in Stockholm, King Gustavus of Sweden dubbed Thorpe "the greatest athlete in the world." He had stunned everyone with victories in the two most demanding track and field events, the Pentathalon and the Decathalon. Tewanima received the silver for second place in both the 5,000 and 10,000 meter races.

Back at home Thorpe and Tewanima were less successful. Relieved of his Olympic honors for having played semi-pro baseball during a summer prior to the games, Thorpe dropped into relative obscurity. Three years before he died in 1953 he was named by an Associated Press poll of sportswriters as "the greatest American Athlete of the first half of this century." Twenty years after his death the Amateur Athletic Union restored his awards in the Olympic books.

Tewanima returned to a quiet life as a traditional Hopi farmer and Antelope Society priest. According to Fred Kabotie, his performance at a home-state race seemed almost a contest between native and white styles of training. "I know him," Kabotie said. "He was to take part in a marathon on the Fourth of July. My uncle and I rode there on burros. We camped at night on the way. We were in the Winslow grandstand and there was Louis, and about three other Hopi runners, not Carlisle students, and Zuni runners with animal fetishes to give them strength which they held the entire race. When they started Louis was out in front by a long stretch. About the third round, the Hopi runners passed him up, then the Zunis passed him up. He didn't even finish. It turned out Pop Warner's training didn't do any good against those Hopi runners."

In the 1920s long distance races became widely promoted in the United States with some of the hoopla of professional wrestling; Indian contestants were an exotic addition. In 1925 Louis Tewanima was lured from Arizona to run in the highly-publicized New York to California "Bunion Derby." He took first place, but was disqualified for an infraction of the rules. One source has suggested that the ease and speed of his performance deflated audience interest. When he was eighty years old Tewanima was still walking twenty miles a day to herd sheep. Ten years later he died from a fall off the cliff at Shungopavi.

In both 1927 and 1928 Karok Indians from northern California were winners of the 480-mile Grants Pass run, from Sausalito, California to Grant's Pass, Oregon, a celebration of the Redwood Highway. After his 1928 victory Henry Thomas took the name "Flying Cloud" from the Pierce automobile he received as first prize. In 1927 a forty-three-year-old Oneida, "Chief" Tall Feather, broke the record for a non-stop "marathon" from Milwaukee to Chicago, 94 miles in 19 hours and 47 minutes. In 1926 and 1927 a Detroit Indian youth, Chauncey Longwhite, made news first winning the ten-mile Patasonia race in Chicago, then winning the four-mile Chicago Daily News Race in 19:41.

Those years also produced Indian athletes from the southwest. The Zuni Andrew Chimony ran a twelve-mile "Ceremonial Race" at Gallup, New Mexico in 1926. Despite having to forge through a sandstorm for the first four miles, he came out thirty seconds behind the record made at Madison Square Garden. The following year he went to New York to win a twelve-mile "modified marathon." In a pack of 186 of America's top runners he finished a quarter-mile in front. Also in 1927, Nicholas Quanawahu, one of Tewanima's fellow tribesmen, beat out 234 runners to win the full-length Long Beach Marathon.

The next Indian personality to make running news was a Narragansett tribesman named Ellison M. "Tarzan" Brown. Brown was twenty years old when he appeared out of Alton, Rhode Island to participate in the 1935 Boston Marathon clad in a running tunic sewn by his sisters from his dead mother's dress. The following year he staggered everyone by winning the Boston Marathon and earning a place at that summer's Olympics in Germany.

Brown always displayed a cavalier attitude towards training, and began the Berlin marathon with only nine days of preparation. For eighteen miles he held the lead, then a muscle cramp forced him to take a massage stop and a spectator came to his aid. He was disqualified. Amidst heckling back home he decided to "show them Ellison Brown is no quitter." Brazenly he signed up for a spectacular effort, two full length marathons that October, in Port Chester, New York, and Manchester, New Hampshire—within the same twenty-four-hour time period. He won them both.

Ellison "Tarzan" Brown winning the 1939 Boston Marathon

A free spirit, Brown was seen wolfing down a hot dog before a race because he'd forgotten breakfast; he boasted that chopping wood and quitting beer were his workouts. He interrupted one Boston Marathon with a plunge into the enticing waters of Lake Cochituate, waving on fellow competitors. In 1939, however, he took the Boston championship in a record 2:28:51.8. Brown's life ended on the same sort of downbeat which attended Thorpe and Longboat. He went through a series of odd jobs, sold his trophies to pay for groceries and medical bills for foot injuries stemming from his running, and was killed by a car after an argument in a bar.

Tarahumaras were also included in the flurry of excitement over Indians running in long distance races. Initially their performances were auspicious. In 1927 two of them ran the 89.4 miles from San Antonio to Austin, Texas in 14:53. Another Tarahumara, Jose Torres, broke an 1882 record when he covered the 51 miles from Kansas City to Lawrence in 6:46:41. He and fellow Tarahumara, Aurelio Terrazas, entered the Amsterdam Olympics the next year. Running for Mexico, they paced themselves for the cross-country runs of home. Apparently no one made it clear to them that marathons were only 26 miles, 385 yards long. Minutes behind the front runners, the Tarahumaras crossed the finish line and continued running until halted by officials. "Too short, too short," they complained.

It seemed the Tarahumaras, as with other Indians, found it difficult to extract their running prowess from its cultural context and reshape it to fit the white man's criteria for competitive sports. According to writer Michael Jenkinson, who joined Karl Kernberger on his trips to Chihuahua, their metabolism could not make the adjustment from their normal diet of *kovisiki,* pinole or corn gruel, to a training program of eggs, milk and beefsteak. At home they shunned the fried foods of their Mexican neighbors, preferring roasted or boiled foods. Nor did they much like meat, sweets or fat. Running in endless circles bored them. These races gave them bad dreams, they said. The cleated leather shoes required at Olympic meets did not conform to their splayed, bark-hard feet. The scrutiny of howling strangers contrasted with the support of backers and friends at home and the winding stretches of quiet mountain trails.

Apart from cultural contrasts the question lurked whether intrinsic physical or metabolic superiorities enabled the Tarahumara, the Hopi, the Zuni and others to run so long and well. *"L'homme civilize ne connait pas ses forces,"* wrote Georges Comte de Buffon in 1749 ("Civilized man does not know his powers"). But the white man often preferred to imagine that primitive peoples possessed different bodies as well as developed skills.

With the exception of a few Tarahumara studies, the physiological investigation of Indian running has been confined to anecdotal observation. In 1921 Dr. Henry Craig Fleming, attached

to the Hendricks-Hodge anthropological expedition, witnessed a
Zuni kick-stick race. When eight of the runners returned from the
grueling run, over fifteen miles, they were bathed in perspiration.
Fleming was astonished that they "revealed comparatively no
evidence of fatigue, no respiratory distress, and no heart rate above
106 beats per minute." Nor did they betray any of the characteristic
symptoms of the "psychological syndrome of effort": dilated
nostrils, breathlessness, stiffness, consciousness of heart beat. He
was also amazed at the endurance level of men in their seventies
whose blood pressure was as low as men half their age.

In 1975 journalist James Norman visited the Tarahumara and
climbed up to an isolated community named Guagueybo. During
his hike he was passed by a runner who had already gone up and
down the mountain once. Norman compared their pulse rates: his
own was 170, the Tarahumara's, 70. Medical study has suggested
that long distance success depends upon "running economy and the
ability to utilize a large fraction of a well-developed aerobic
capacity." Many of the Indian folktales about running are lessons in

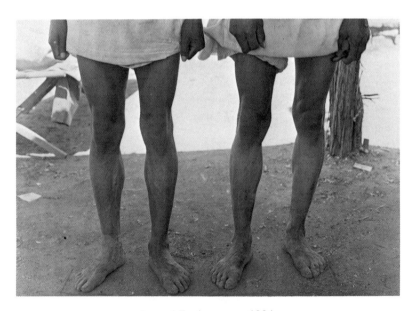

Legs of Zuni runners, 1921

such economy and pacing. To explore the endurance capabilities of Indians, two Oklahoma biodynamic researchers visited the Tarahumara in the fall of 1963 and spring of 1964.

While the Tarahumara kick-ball runners tested expended energy at the "upper limits of human voluntary work effort," the more acculturated Tarahumara boys in a Mission boarding school did not demonstrate an aerobic capacity much different from their Mexican or mixed-blood classmates. The people's running feats seemed the result of conditioning rather than genetic adaptation. This view was strengthened a few years later when Italian physiologists from Milan compared running and non-running Tarahumaras. While the runners showed a maximum aerobic power equal to that of professional athletes, non-runners tested well below them. The researchers also learned that former runners retained the "stroke volume"—the strength of the heart's contraction—of active runners.

This suggested that it was the running life, and not mysterious gifts of nature, which gave the Tarahumara their deserved reputation. But more study is warranted. These researchers looked at the lungs and heart, however, little research has been devoted to studying the average allocation of "short twitch" and "long twitch" muscles in running tribes. It has been suggested that Indians may possess a higher percentage of the "short twitch" muscle fibers which provide the slower contraction needed to sustain effort for long distances. Most of us have equal shares of these fiber types, but the legs of natural marathoners, like Bill Rodgers, reveal up to eighty percent "short twitch" muscles. What about Indians?

For Pueblo runners who tried to make the transition from traditional running to sports competition, a single-minded emphasis on training and victory could mean that those who won on the outside were in jeopardy of becoming losers within the community. Perhaps this is why the greatest Indian track star of recent times was not a Pueblo athlete but an Oglala Sioux who had been orphaned at the age of thirteen. At the 1964 Olympics in Tokyo, the ex-Marine Billy Mills ran against thirty-six of the greatest racers in the world for the 10,000 meter event. During the final 300 yards he was accidently pushed by another runner and fell behind twenty yards. But he rebounded to win by .04 of a second, beating Louis Tewanima's record with his 28:24:04 time.

In his controversial article baring the problems of Indian runners, *Sports Illustrated* correspondent Bertram Gabriel claimed that Pueblo athletes had a harder time staying on top. Although he disliked the tone and many of the assumptions of the piece, Bruce Talawema agreed that the Indian runners in school did experience homesickness and felt an acute need to touch base frequently with the social and ceremonial life of the community and family. ''Kids today still feel obligated to help out their family,'' coach Emmett

Billy Mills at finish line, Tokoyo Olympics, 1964

188

Generations of Jemez runners. From left to right: Felipe Waquie, early 1900s; Juanito Sando 1914; Joe Sando, 1939.

Hunt told *Sports Illustrated.* "In the family if someone is sick, everybody is there. If you have to get off work, you get off work. If you lose your job, you lose it, but you're there. All the people I grew up with are still in Laguna." Taking a more critical view, Acoma runner Gary Louis told Gabriel, "Some of our people get kind of jealous of anybody who's really achieving something. They cut you down a lot . . . I've thought a lot about why Indian athletes don't go on. There's Jim Thorpe and Billy Mills, period. Indians make a name for themselves in high school, and the next thing you know they're pumping gas."

At one Pueblo, however, the Indian and white man's styles of running seem to have meshed compatibly. "Jemez Pueblo has had a history of racing and running," Joe Sando told me proudly. "As kids we heard stories about our famous runners. In the late 1800s there were Pablo Gachupin and a man named Fragua. They were followed by Felipe Waquie, father of Felix and grandfather of Al, who told me that he ran against the Hopi Tewanima, at the University of New Mexico around 1910."

In 1958 Sando helped launch the village's "All Indian Track Meet" every Father's Day, which has come to include runners from tribes across the west. Jemez has continued to produce stunning run-

189

Al Waquie at second annual Po'pay Race, San Juan Pueblo, 20 July 1980

ners from its famous athletic families. Steve Gachupin won the twenty-eight-mile Pike's Peak road race six times in the 1960s. Al Waquie, a firefighter by profession, has made his reputation on the brutal nine-mile race to the 10,678-foot summit of the Sandia Crest. Known as the La Luz Trail, it climbs from Sandia Pueblo at about 5,000 feet elevation up the west face of the mountain into a sub-alpine zone, where temperatures can fall fifty degrees lower than in Albuquerque below. For the last four years the race has been Waquie's personal property, with his 1980 time his best—1:12:40. Since its experience with the Tricentennial Run, Jemez appears to have continued symbolic meets; earlier this year it held a special run to galvanize community action against geothermal development in the Jemez Mountains.

Over the last decade other Indian peoples have organized successful running tournaments, some commemorative, some for training purposes, most with the key ingredient of communal participation. In Yakima, Washington, the Plateau tribes hold their Kiutus Jim Thirteen Kilometer run, which is now a fixture of their week-long Toppenish Creek Encampment in mid-summer. The Hopi held their eighth Annual Louis Tewanima Memorial Foot Race last year. Since 1978 urban Indians in California have repeated the Spiritual Run which began as a show of support for the Longest Walk demonstration against anti-Indian legislation then pending in Congress. A product of the sophisticated organizing of Oakland's Inter-tribal Friendship House, this year it again saw Indians running 500 miles from Davis to Los Angeles.

Another Indian running event born in 1978 was a special camp for Indian runners held in Boulder, Colorado and sponsored by the University of Colorado's American Indian Educational Opportunity Program. For five days twenty-five high school runners and five state champions, representing eighteen different tribes, were exposed to workshops and lectures by such running greats as Frank Shorter and Billy Mills. Its goal was the enhancement of Indian athletics on the national level. Bruce Gomez—who had taken the Tricentennial pouch from Taos—wrote after his participation in the intensive workshop, "It is the first time that young Indian runners of different tribes have been put together in a cohesive training-oriented environment to receive training expertise and encouragement to develop their God-given talents. Personally it was a dream come true."

Near my apartment in Berkeley, the telephone poles are laminated with posters advertising many kinds of physical and psychological therapies. I unpeeled a recent layer promoting workshops in "vision quests," weekends devoted to "living your own myth and inventing rituals for your life" and varieties of do-it-yourself "shamanism." Unlike other societies, Indians have generally not felt the need to proselytize their beliefs, but it is probable that their running ways will become candidates for this sort of conversion out of context. If white runners wanted to build a bridge from ritual to romance out of their own heritage they could hearken to ancient Rome, where the Luperci, worshippers of Faunus, the Roman Pan, would hold a ceremonial run around the Palatine Mount. In their hands were thongs from the skin of freshly sacrificed goats; the running was an act of purification. Or, to ancient Greece, where a rite known as "the running around" saw babies carried at a run around the family hearth, possibly to bless them in the currents of air around the flame—a ritual remarkably similar to the baptismal action of the

Pomo father who would run with his newborn in his hands to greet the first full moon following birth.

But it is to Indians that our imagination turns, to brew imitative magic from tribal ritual. Already runners have been spotted on the Berkeley campus with *Chasqui* printed on their T-shirts. In San Diego, reports Valerie Andrews, author of *The Psychic Power of Running,* a group holds Tarahumara-style *Tesguinadas* in Torrey Pines, while in La Jolla a "tribe" runs with flaming torches along the beaches during the summer solstice. In part this is in healthy reaction to the solitary, self-improvement fixation of some running devotees, who seem engaged in what Newsweek columnist Meg Greenfield described as "a personal endurance test, not something that has to do with the general well-being of the group." They are searching for something more than the loneliness of the long distance runner.

But as they look they should heed some Hopi advice heard by Alexander M. Stephen in 1885. Wicki, the Antelope Society Chief at Walpi on First Mesa, delivered one of Spider Woman's prophecies. "A time would come," he told Stephen "when men with white skins and a strange tongue would join the Hopi. Because they had brave hearts the Snake priests would be the first to make friends and learn from them." But the Hopi, Spider Woman was said to urge, were not to follow in the white man's footsteps, they should move beside them. It was in the footsteps of their fathers that they should walk. And, Spider Woman might have added, run.

Perhaps it is possible to reach beyond the superficial, over-simplified imitation of Indian running and still be inspired by its spirit and motivation. Recent interest in "orienteering" and wilderness runs, optimal performance training, and the "inner" aspect of running represent this direction, and conform more to the Hopi and Navajo values of a running life. These ancient American traditions of people in fast motion help to dignify our hunger to cover ground in participation with what scholar of religions Mircea Eliade calls "the cosmic totality." For I suspect that in some way all runners share the yearning expressed in the Navajo chant:

The mountain, I become part of it . . .
The herbs, the fir tree,
I become part of it.
The morning mists,
The clouds, the gathering waters,
I become part of it.
The sun that sweeps across the earth,
I become part of it.
The wilderness, the dew drops, the pollen . . .
I become part of it.

Acknowledgements

I am grateful to Stewart Brand of *Co-Evolution Quarterly* for encouraging Margaret MacLean and myself to write the cover story, "Ways of Native American Running," (Summer 1980) which opened me up to this topic. When the book project came along, Margaret graciously turned over our material to me. Most of that piece has been incorporated into this book.

I owe special thanks to Alfonso Ortiz for supporting my coverage of the Tricentennial Run and my research with tips and enthusiasm, and I am indebted to the other American Indian people who have encouraged me along the way, especially Herman Agoyo, Rex Lee Jim, Fred Kabotie and Joe Sando.

My gratitude to the following scholars, librarians and friends who have been extremely helpful: Karol Andrews, Sam and Janet Bingham, Thomas Buckley, Ward Churchill, William N. Fenton, Ray Fogelson, Diana Fane, Gerrit Fenenga, Hazel W. Hertzberg, Laura Holt, James N. Howard, Dee Travis Hudson, Mike Kakuska, John MacAloon, Tracy McCallum, Leslie Navari, Dolores Newton, Triloki Pandey, Joan Pursell, John H. Rowe, William Sagstetter, William Simmons, William C. Sturtevant, Jeffrey Whitmore, Abbie Lou Williams, Terry Wilson, Clee Woods.

To Kit Tremaine I owe particular thanks for encouragement and support.

Notes on Sources

This documentary montage on Indian running has been assembled from writings and statements by a host of anthropologists, historians, linguists, travellers and Indians themselves, and by no means exhausts the literature on Indian running. At critical points in the text, and in this list of only the major works I used, I hope my great debt to their efforts is made crystal clear. Since my overall story and use of their material is for the general reader, I have chosen not to clutter the book with footnotes, preferring to let each chapter's principal research unfold in this narrative bibliography. Where I have incorporated substantial quotes I have added page references. When rendering words from Indian vocabularies I have not attempted to standardize their orthography, preferring to copy the spelling [and diacritical marks] of my sources.

After the initial research which Margaret MacLean and I conducted largely at Santa Fe's Laboratory of Anthropology, my literature search took a quantum leap as I delved into the cross-referenced index and microfiche of New Haven's Human Relations Area Files (HRAF) at U.C. Santa Barbara. Under codings for "athletic sports," "spectacles," and "recreation" I located numerous references to running. With my probe into the University of California's *Culture Element Distribution* (*American Archaeology and Ethnology,* and *Anthropological Records*, Berkeley: UC Press, 1935-1950), at Santa Barbara's Museum of Natural History, stories about running among Indian cultures outside the Southwest then became available.

For background on the Southwest Pueblo Indians and the region's geography I relied on the Writer's Project guide, *New Mexico: A Guide to the Colorful State* (New York: Hastings House, revised 1953), the Smithsonian's new *Southwest* (*Handbook of North American Indians,* V. 9, Washington: Smithsonian, 1979), Henry F. Dobyns and Robert C. Euler's *Indians of the Southwest: A Critical Bibliography* (Bloomington: Indiana University, 1980), and the aerial photos and village plans of Stanley A. Stubbs' *Bird's-Eye View of the Pueblos* (Norman: University of Oklahoma, 1950) which helped me to retrace our steps following the Tricentennial runners in and out of these towns.

For information on Pueblo ceremonialism and commentary on running, Elsie Clews Parsons' monumental *Pueblo Indian Religion* (Chicago: University of Chicago, 1939) was invaluable; the two-volume culmination of a quarter-century of fieldwork is referred to here as Parsons (PIR). The useful compilations of Hamilton A. Tyler, all published by University of Oklahoma: *Pueblo Gods and Myths* (1964), *Pueblo Animals and Myths* (1975), and *Pueblo Birds and Myths* (1979) became a sort of cross-index to Parsons. Popular sources on the Pueblo people which contained running details were Frank Waters' *Masked Gods* (New York:

Hopi runner, ca. 1915

196

Ballantine, 1970) and Vincent Scully's impressionistic *Pueblo: Mountain, Village, Dance* (New York: Viking, 1972). Ruth Underhill's *Workaday Life of the Pueblos* (Bureau of Indian Affairs, 1954), although a pamphlet for young people was equally rich in running facts.

In researching Indian games I encountered references to stick games, a favorite pastime of women and men in over sixty tribes. Space limitations prevented me from including "shinny" or "lacrosse" data even though those sports involved ceaseless running. I did, however, use James Mooney's material on Cherokee magic for ball game runners.

Sources on the Pueblo Revolt include Charles Wilson Hackett's *Revolt of the Pueblo Indians of New Mexico* (Albuquerque: University of New Mexico, 1942) and Ralph Emerson Twitchell's *Leading Facts of New Mexican History* (Cedar Rapids: The Torch Press, 1911). More popular accounts, such as Franklin Folsom's *Red Power on the Rio Grande* (Chicago: Follett, 1973), Robert Silverberg's more extensive *The Pueblo Revolt* (New York: Weybright and Talley, 1970), the special newspaper features during the Tricentennial *(Albuquerque Journal,* August 3, 1980), and briefer versions such as Joseph Sando's "The Pueblo Revolt" in *Southwest* (Washington: Smithsonian, 1979) are largely reconstructed from the Spanish documents collected in those works. Folsom's map using the original Pueblo names was helpful, and Sando's blend of the Indian record with the Spanish version was a relief. More recently, Alfonso Ortiz' "The Pueblo Revolt of 1680: In Commemoration" *(A Ceremony of Brotherhood.* Albuquerque: Academia Press, 1981) also makes sense of the Revolt from the Pueblo Perspective.

CHAPTER ONE

Willa Cather portrays Zuni runners in *Death Comes for the Archbishop,* (New York: Vintage, 1971, p. 235). Bertha Dutton mentions Santo Domingo Corn Dance runners in her summary, *Indians of the American Southwest* (Englewood Cliffs: Prentice-Hall, 1975). Apache knotted cords are mentioned in J. G. Bourke's *Medicine Men of the Apache* (Washington: Bureau of American Ethnology, Annual Report 9, 1892), while in California E. M. Loeb learned of their use among the Pomo *(Pomo Folkways,* Berkeley: University Publications in American Archeology and Ethnology, 19, 1926). Po'pay's inspiration for the knotted cord is from J. Walter Fewkes' "Documentary History of the Zuni Tribe" (Cambridge: The Riverside Press, 1892, p. 112).

I was led to Truman Michelson's extraordinary find, "Notes on the Ceremonial Runners of the Fox Indians" *(Contributions to Fox Ethnology,* Washington: Bureau of American Ethnology, Bull. 85, 1927, pp. 1-50) by James H. Howard. Carobeth Laird's account of Southern California's ceremonial runners is in *The Chemehuevis* (Morongo: Malki Museum, 1976), while Walter Goldschmidt's *Nomlaki Ethnography* (Berkeley: University of California, 1951) mentions "newsboys" further north in California. Goldschmidt adds details on running in hand-to-hand combat. Donna Preble's *Yamino-Kwiti: Boy Runner of Siba*

(Caldwell: Caxton Printers, 1948) was a glorious discovery, stamped as it was with a seal of approval from Alfred Kroeber who says, "I know of no full-length piece of fiction concerned with the American Indian that is in better conformity with the ethnological facts." At the same time I located D'Arcy McNickle's work of juvenile fiction *Runner In the Sun* (Toronto: John C. Winston, 1954) which describes an Anasazi boy's prehistoric run to Mexico in search of a new strain of maize. John G. Bourke in *Journal of American Folklore* (July, Sept. 1889) offers a traveller's aside on Mohave runners while Paul H. Ezell's "The Cocomaricopa Mail" (San Diego: Corral of the Westerners, Brand Book No. 1, 1968) pictures Yuman couriers in their heyday.

I first learned of Iroquois runners from Hazel Hertzberg's splendid exposition of Iroquois culture and world view, *The Great Tree and the Longhouse* (New York: Macmillan, 1966). William N. Fenton then traced for me the actual route followed by their relays, and directed me to the James Emlen journal entry *(Ethnohistory,* V. 12, Fall 1965). Lewis Henry Morgan emphasized the foot messengers' importance to the Iroquois Confederacy in *League of the Ho-De-No-Sau-Nee or Iroquois* (New York, 1901).

Victor Von Hagen's *World of the Maya* (New York: New American Library, 1960) mentions Mayan roads, while William H. Prescott's *History of the Conquest of Mexico and*

History of the Conquest of Peru (New York: The Modern Library, N.D. pp. 29-30), describes Aztec runners. To piece together the Peruvian courier system my mainstay was John H. Rowe's "Inca Culture at the Time of the Spanish Conquest" (Washington: Bureau of American Ethnology, Bull. 143, 1946). In HRAF at Santa Barbara I also obtained pertinent pages from these early Spanish chroniclers: Polo de Ondegardo (c. 1545), Pedro de Cienza de Leon (1541-1550), Garcilaso de la Vega (c. 1555), and don Felipe Guaman Poma de Ayala (c. 1613), whose visual coverage of Peruvian cultural history includes a chasqui (Nuevos Coronicos y Buen Cobierno. Paris: Institut d'Ethnologie, Traveau et Memoirs, V. 23, 1936). Wendell C. Bennett's reference to runner depictions on Mochica pottery is in "The Andean Highlands: An Introduction" (Washington: Smithsonian Bull. 143, V. 2, 1944) and they are shown in Christopher B. Donnan's Moche Art of Peru: Pre-Columbian Symbolic Communication (Los Angeles: Museum of Cultural History, 1978).

Accounts of Hopi long distance messenger runs come from George W. James' The Indians of the Painted Desert Region (Boston: Little, Brown, 1903), Walter Hough's The Hopi Indians (Cedar Rapids: The Torch Press, 1915, pp. 108-110), and Edward S. Curtis' V. 12, The Hopi, of his twenty-volume The North American Indian (Norwood, 1922, p. 52). Charlie Talawepi's run was recalled in a Berkeley coffee house by his grandson, Roy Albert (3 Nov. 1980). In Blanche Grant's The Taos Indians (Glorieta: Rio Grande, 1976 reprint) there is an account of an even longer mission: Taos runner Mauricio Martinez was hired to deliver a message by foot to Kansas City.

For foot racing mythology, one or two stories in almost every tribe's folklore exploit the running contest motif. In a Zuni tale told Anna Rissler, "Seven Zuni Folktales" (El Palacio, Santa Fe: Oct. 1941), a first race decided that women would be more beautiful than men, a second that the most beautiful women would have the homeliest husbands. Of many versions of the race dividing men from animals is the Cheyenne tale in Alice Marriott and Carol K. Rachlin's American Indian Mythology (New York: Thomas Y. Crowell, 1968).

Racing as a means for determining how the world will look and function is found in

such California collections as A. H. Gayton and Stanley S. Newman's Yokuts and Western Mono Myths (Berkeley: Anthropological Records, V. 5, 1940). Roland Dixon's Maidu Myths (New York: American Museum of Natural History, Bull. 17, 1902) contains one of many stories in which racing allocates animals to their habits. Tribes from the Yokuts to the Yumans and beyond connected the Milky Way with these decisive, primordial races. The Mayan Genesis story is in Ralph L. Roy's "A Maya Account of the Creation" (American Anthropologist, n.s. 22, 1920). Perhaps the favorite race motif concerns a Trickster figure who feigns lameness; in Stith Thompson's Tales of the North American Indians (Bloomington: Indiana University, 1966) versions are cited from throughout the Plains and Southwest. Slow animals beating faster ones is another popular plot, contained in such collections as John R. Swanton's Myths and Tales of the Southeastern Indians (Washington: Bureau of American Ethnology, Bull. 88, 1929).

The Hopi priest's spellbinding account of ritual running is in the remarkable diary kept by the Scotsman, Alexander M. Stephen, who lived in Hopiland in the 1880's; Hopi Journal (New York: Columbia Contributions to Anthropology, 23, 1936, p. 780). I quote from Margot Astrov's "The Concept of Motion as the Psychological Leitmotif of Navaho Life and Literature" (Journal of American Folklore, Jan.-March, 1950). Appropriating Joe Sachs' paraphrase of Aristotle ("Aristotle's definition of Motion," The College, St. Johns College, Annapolis, Jan. 1976), I tied it into Lucien Lévy-Bruhl's "primitive participation" discussion in The Notebooks on Primitive Mentality (New York: Harper & Rowe, 1975; Aug.-Sept. 1938).

Throughout the Tricentennial Run, Tom Kavanagh, Tricentennial Coordinator for the Hopi Tribe, gave interviews, headed us toward the pass to intercept runners, and after the event answered my written and phoned queries. I owe him a great debt. I quote from Herman Agoyo's reminiscence in "The Tricentennial Year in Pueblo Consciousness" (El Palacio, Winter, 1980-1981). For comparative analysis of public ritual I dug into Ronald L. Grimes' Symbol and Conquest: Public Ritual and Drama in Santa Fe, New Mexico (Ithaca: Cornell University, 1976). Fortunately, on 18 March 1980, I interviewed the Hopi painter Fred Kabotie, and that discussion helped to hold the *Co-Evolution Quarterly* article together in addition to introducing me to key themes of Indian running and the upcoming Tricentennial Run.

CHAPTER TWO

The best ethnographic study of Taos is Elsie Clews Parsons' *Taos Pueblo* (Menasha: General Series in Anthropology, 2, 1936, pp. 96-97. Alfonso Ortiz' interpretation of Tewa relays is in "Ritual Drama and the Pueblo World View" *(New Perspectives on the Pueblos,* Albuquerque: University of New Mexico, 1972, pp. 151-153). Taos running folklore is from Elsie Claws Parsons' *Taos Tales* (New York: American Folklore Society, 1940, pp. 48-49, 105-106), Edward S. Curtis' *The Tiwa (The North American Indian* V. 16, Norwood, 1926, p. 60), and Elizabeth W. DeHuff's *Taytay's Memories* New York: Harcourt, Brace, 1924).

Taos librarian Tracy McCallum wrote me about the San Geronimo Day relay races of 1980, and alerted me to Joseph Foster's description in *D. H. Lawrence in Taos* (Albuquerque: University of New Mexico, 1972). Lawrence's essay is in *Mornings in Mexico* (New York: Alfred A. Knopf, 1927, pp. 121-122). N. Scott Momaday's gripping description is in *House Made of Dawn* (Perennial Library, 1977, p. 191) and Frank Waters' evocation of the Taos relays is in *The Man Who Killed the Deer* (Pocket Books, 1971, pp. 204-206).

The most detailed study of any Indian running ceremony is Morris E. Opler's "The Jicarilla Apache Ceremonial Relay Race" *(American Anthropologist,* n.s. V. 46, 1944). The extent of California Indian "new moon" racing is suggested in Philip Drucker's *Culture Element Distribution* list (Berkeley: Anthropological Records, 1, 1937), while John P. Harrington's edition of A. Robinson's translation of Father Geronimo Boscana's writings *(Chinigchinich,* Santa Ana: Fine Arts Press, 1933, p. 173-174) contains a first-hand account along with Harrington's personal aside. Alfred Kroeber's *Handbook of the Indians of California* (Berkeley: Dover reprint, 1976) is replete with references to Indian running songs, running ritual, and famous long-distance races.

Background on Tewa running was gathered from "Ceremonial Racing" in Elsie Clews Parsons' *The Social Organization of the Tewa of New Mexico* (Memoirs: American Anthropological Assn., V. 36, 1929). My San Juan Pueblo description was abetted by Alfonso Ortiz' classic *The Tewa World* (Chicago: University of Chicago, 1969) and Ortiz' quote from *Look to the Mountaintop* (San Jose: Gousha Press, 1972).

CHAPTER THREE

For material on the Keres-speaking world I relied on Charles Lange's solid *Cochiti* (Austin: University of Texas, 1959) and works of anthropologist Leslie White. Approaching the secretive Pueblos like a cultural sleuth, White produced a series of community profiles; from his *The Pueblo of Santo Domingo* (Memoirs: American Anthropological Assn., 43, 1935) I took the basic story of the Bloody Kachina. Edward S. Curtis' *Keres (The North American Indian,* V. 16, Norwood, 1926) described Santo Domingo's runner kachinas, while his *Hopi* volume and Ruth Benedict's *Tales of the Cochiti Indians* (Washington: Bureau of Ethnology, Bull. 98, 1931) demonstrated how tribal versions of a piece of lore can differ. Twitchell (1911, p. 366, footnote #375) reports the perhaps apocryphal Zia (or Jemez) story of the killing of the priest.

Mischa Titiev's comment on the practical origins of ritual running is in *The Hopi Indians of Old Oraibi* (Ann Arbor: University of Michigan, 1972, p. 226), while Stewart Culin's different view is in his definitive *Games of the North American Indians* (Washington: Bureau of American Ethnology, 24th Annual Report, 1907). Diana Fane, assistant curator at the Brooklyn Museum filled me in on Culin's career (personal communication, 7 Oct. 1980). Parsons (PIR, pp. 820-821) presented the Hopi interpretations of running which Stephen had collected.

My medley of runners' supernatural aids and names comes from many sources, notably James Mooney's "The Cherokee Ball Play" *(American Anthropologist,* April, 1980) and Buffalo Bird Woman's life story (Bismark: *North Dakota History,* Winter/Spring 1971). For Jemez running and racing I owe profound gratitude to Indian scholar Joe Sando whose personal communication (18 Nov. 1980), and unpublished and published writings ("Indian Olympics," *New Mexico,* April 1952) I incorporated with material from Elsie Clews Parsons' *The Pueblo of Jemez* (New Haven: Yale University, 1925). Robert Coles' gift for extracting children's memories and feelings is revealed in his *Eskimos, Chicanos, Indians* (Boston: Little Brown, 1977). The Isleta material comes again from Parsons: *Isleta, New Mexico* (Washington: Bureau of American Ethnology, 47th Annual Report, 1932).

For running and hunting I used G. M. Foster's "A Summary of Yuki Culture" (Berkeley: Anthropological Records, 5, 1944), W. W. Hill's *The Agricultural and Hunting Methods of the Navaho Indians* (New Haven: Yale University, 1938), the personal account of Albert B. Reagan, "The Jemez Indians" *(El Palacio,* April 1917), Edith H. Wilson's quote from Cochiti in "Enemy Bear" (Los Angeles: *The Masterkey,* Southwest Museum, May 1948), and the story of the Omaha "buffalo runners" from Alice C. Fletcher and Francis La Flesche's *The Omaha Tribe* (Lincoln: V. 2, University of Nebraska, 1972).

CHAPTER FOUR

I found Schoolcraft's journal entry in Part Four of his *Information Respecting . . . the Indian Tribes of the United States* (Philadelphia: Lippincott, Grambo, 1854). The report on Pueblo trackmen today, Bertram Gabriel's "Running to Nowhere." *(Sports Illustrated,* Nov. 16, 1979), mentioned here is discussed further in chapter eight. The Osage running track is in Tillie K. Newman's *The Black Dog Trail,* (Kansas: Bicentennial Project, 1976). The Eskimo running material comes from Edward S. Curtis' *Eskimo (The North American Indian,* V. 20, Norwood, 1930) and the Charles C. Hughes' life history of the man he calls "Nathan Kalkianak," *Eskimo Boyhood* (Lexington: University of Kentucky, 1974, pp. 115-116). Ruth Landes' *The Ojibwa Woman* (New York: AMS Press, 1969 reprint, pp. 22-26) told Part-Sky-Woman's story.

Unfortunately there was no room to do justice to Plains Indian running, in such rituals as the Crow Tobacco Society ceremony as well as in war training and sport. The Cheyenne tale of the elderly Little Wolf was in Thomas B. Marquis' *Wooden Leg: A Warrior Who Fought Custer* (Lincoln: University of Nebraska, 1962).

Clee Woods of Albuquerque, once a long distance runner at Marshall University, has observed many Southwestern Indian races; his "Indian Track Meet" *(New Mexico,* March 1946) and a personal communication (26 Oct. 1980) helped me enjoy them also. The other Isleta material comes again from the Parsons 1932 monograph and from her *Isleta Paintings* (Washington: Bureau of American Ethnology, Bull 181, 1962).

Curt Nimuendaju's *The Eastern Timbira* (Berkeley: University Publications in American Archeology and Ethnology, 1946, pp. 136-143) led me into Brazilian Indian "log-running," and then John H. Rowe of U.C. Berkeley directed me to Vilma Schultz' "Indians of Central Brazil" in *Vanishing Peoples of the Earth* (Washington: National Geographic Society, 1968), Robert Lowie's "Northwestern and Central Ge" *(Handbook of South American Indians,* V. 1, Bureau of American Ethnology, Bull. 143, 1946), and David Maybury-Lewis' *The Savage and the Innocent* (Cleveland: World, 1965, pp. 86-87). Anthropologist Dolores Newton's personal communications (2 Jan. 1981, 4 March 1981), plus her photos brought the account up to date. Dr. Rowe also graciously gave me access to Nimuendaju's negatives.

Charles Lummis' *Pueblo Indian Folk-Stories* (New York: Century, 1910) contains both the Coyote and Rabbit race and its real-life counterpart. I thank Bruce Talawema for talking on 8 August 1980 about his own running career and participation in the Tricentennial.

CHAPTER FIVE

Diana Fane of the Brooklyn Museum sent me Stewart Culin's unpublished field notes from his Zuni sojourn in 1903. The writings of Frank Hamilton Cushing *(Zuni Breadstuff,* New York: Museum of American Indian, 1920), *(Zuni Creation Myths,* Washington: Bureau of American Ethnology, 13th Report, 1896), *(Zuni Folk Tales,* New York: G. P. Putnam's sons, 1901), and M. C. Stevenson's summary, "Zuni Games" *(American Anthropologist,* n.s. 5, 1903) were vital to my understanding of kick-stick racing, as were F. W. Hodge's "A Zuni Foot Race" *(American Anthropologist,* July 1980), and the social background and religious map of the Pueblo in Alfred L. Kroeber's *Zuni Kin and Clan* (New York: American Museum of Natural History Anthro. Papers, 1917).

Triloki Pandey of U.C. Santa Cruz pointed me to John G. Owens' "Some

Hopi ceremonial runner, 1901

Games of the Zuni" *(Popular Science Monthly,* V. 39, 1891). The numerous accounts of Zuni kick-stick races end with Roy Keech's "The Kick-stick race at Zuni" *El Palacio,* N. 37, 1934, pp. 61-64). I am especially grateful to Louis Tsethlikai for recalling his kick-stick experiences. For Keres-speaking traditions involving the sport I again depended on Leslie White, both *The Pueblo of Santa Ana* (Memoirs: American Anthropological Assn., N. 60, 1942) and "New Material from Acoma" (Washington: Bureau of American Ethnology, Bull 136, 1943).

The richest source of Papago kick-ball and running ritualism comes from Ruth Underhill, especially *Social Organization of the Papago Indians* (New York: Columbia University Contributions to Anthropology, 30, 1939). Her pamphlet *The Papago Indians of Arizona and their Relatives, the Pima* (Washington: Bureau of Indian Affairs, 1941) and her study of Papago songs, *Singing for Power* (Berkeley: University of California, 1976) I dovetailed with Frank Russell's *The Pima Indians* (Washington: Bureau of American Ethnology, Annual Report 26, 1908) and Leslie Spier's *Yuman Tribes of the Gila River* (Chicago: University of Chicago, 1933) to convey the great kick-ball competitions of a former era. For the esoteric running which climaxed the Papago salt pilgrimage I again relied on Underhill; *Rainhouse and Ocean: Speeches for the Papago Year* (Underhill et al., Flagstaff: Museum of Northern Arizona, 1979) and "The Salt Pilgrimage" (in *Teachings from the American Earth,* New York: Liveright, 1975).

CHAPTER SIX

The Corn Race legend turned up in Edgar L. Hewett's *Ancient Life in the American Southwest* (Indianapolis: Bobbs—Merrill, 1930). I was introduced to the dawn-running of the Navajo through my interview with Rex Lee Jim (6 August 1980). I found other Navaho running lore in Gladys A. Reichard's *Navajo Religion* (Princeton: Bollingen, 1974) and Washington Matthews' "The Night Chant" (New York: Memoirs, American Museum of Natural History, May 1902). I enhanced Rex's account with supporting data and a quote from the famous life-history, Walter Dyk's *Son of Old Man Hat* (Lincoln: University of Nebraska, 1967, HRAF mss. #69-71, Navaho 1-3) and Dorothea Leighton and Clyde Kluckhohn's *Children of the People* (Cambridge: Harvard University Press, 1947).

The foundation of my Apache section i Morris Opler's fascinating *An Apache Lifeway* (New York: Cooper Square, 1965, p. 67), while further war party techniques and customs came from the memories of such old White Mountain Apache fighters as Palmer Valor, found in Keith Basso's edition of Grenville Goodwin's *Western Apache Raiding and Warfare* (Tucson: University of Arizona, 1971). Geronimo's marauding is described both by himself *(Geronimo: His Own Story,* New York: Ballantine Books, 1974) and by Jason Betzinez *(I Fought With Geronimo,* Harrisburg: Stackpole, 1959). Colonel Dodge's comment is from Ernest T. Seton and Julia M. Seton's *The Gospel of the Redman* (Los Angeles: Willing, 1948, pp. 47-49) which offers many Indian running tidbits.

Of the Navajo girl's puberty rite accounts perhaps the most ample is Charlotte J. Frisbie's *Kinaalda: A Study of the Navajo Girl's Puberty Ceremony* (Middletown: Wesleyan University, 1967). An overall study of these ceremonies is Harold Driver's *Girls' Puberty Rites in Western North America* (Berkeley: *Culture Element Distribution,* Anthro. Records, 16, 1941), to which I added, from in-depth accounts from Strong's *Aboriginal Society in Southern California* (Berkeley: University Publications in Archeology and Ethnology, 1929) and Joan Oxendine's "The Luiseno Girl's Ceremony" *(Journal of California and Great Basin Anthropology,* Summer, 1980). For boy's puberty-connected running I used Leslie Spier's *Havasupai Ethnography* (New York: American Museum of Natural History Anthro. Records, V. 29, 1928), Gifford's *The Cocopa* (Berkely: University Publications in American Archeology and Ethnology, V. 31, 1933), and running in datura-drinking ceremonies among Yokuts and Mono is from Harold Driver's *Southern Sierra Nevada* (Berkeley: *Culture Elements Distribution,* Anthro. Records, 6, 1937). The Peruvian *Waracikoy* downhill run is mentioned in Rowe (1946); based, in part, on Cristobal de Molina's account *(Narrative of the Rites and Laws of the Incas,* London: Halkyut Society, 1873).

I am very thankful to Thomas Buckley for his personal communication (23 Oct. 1980) on Yurok running from Northern California, with details evocative of the *lung-gom,* "trance walking," of Tibetan mystics described in Lama Anagrika Govinda's *The*

Way of the White Clouds (Boulder: Shambala, 1970).

CHAPTER SEVEN

To condense my Hopi and Tarahumara profiles from the array of sources, each with its fact or touch of color, was not easy; here I mention only critical research. The bedrock of my Hopi documentation is Stephen (1936), Parsons (PIR), Titiev (1972), and Titiev's synopsis "Hopi Racing Customs at Oraibi" (Ann Arbor: Michigan Academy of Art, Sciences, Letters, V. 24, 1938). Alongside Stephen's and Titiev's day-by-day records of life within the Hopi world, another diary, from the native side, *A Pueblo Journal,* edited by Elsie Clews Parsons (American Anthropological Assn., Memoirs 32, 1921) proved extremely helpful. I drew contemporary quotes from Molly Ivins' "Hopi Spirits Dance Again on the Mesa" *(New York Times,* 30 July 1979). Fred Kabotie's memories brought to life the Snake Dance races, and were reinforced by the photographs of the event in George A. Dorsey and H. R. Voth's *The Mishongnovi Ceremonies of the Snake and Antelope Fraternities* (Chicago: Field Museum Anthro. Series V. 3, 1902), and Robert Black's personal interview (3 Nov. 1980).

In Ernest Beaglehole's work were the kinds of frustrating clues which suggested deeper dimensions of running that I had not time, space, or access to pursue. His "Notes on Hopi Economic Life" (New Haven: Yale Publications in Anthro. N. 15, 1937) noted the Hopi runners of old invading Navajo hogans, while his *The Hopi of Second Mesa* (American Anthropological Assn., N. 44, 1935, p. 46) described the frightening nightly runs of the *Masau* kachina impersonator. Parsons (PIR p. 823) contains the Hopi racing song, and Don Talayesva's two stories are from his autobiography edited by Leo Simmons, *Sun Chief* (New Haven: Yale University, 1942). After I saw the runner kachina doll diorama in the Hopi Cultural Museum, Fred Kabotie described these kachinas in action; then I discovered the fullest study of them in "The Wa-Wac-Ka-Tci-Na, A Tusuyan Foot Race" (Bull. Essex Institute, V. 24, July-Sept. 1892). Among the pictorial guides to kachina costumes and masks, including the runners, is Harold S. Colton's *Hopi Kachina Dolls* (Albuquerque:

University of New Mexico, 1949).

Film-maker Bill Sagstetter kindly sent me his excellent Tarahumara bibliography (personal communications, 9 Oct. 1980, 13 Nov. 1980) and described his experiences among these phenomenal runners. Today's leading scholar is John G. Kennedy; "Contemporary Tarahumara Foot-Racing and its Significance" (Culture Change and Stability, Los Angeles: University of California, 1964, p. 99) and Tarahumara of the Sierra Madre (Illinois: AHM Pub. Corp., 1978). To the many short observations of Tarahumara running, such as Bernard L. Fontana's "Tarahumara: Runners of the West" (Arizona Highways, May 1979), and the longer classics such as Carl Lumholtz' Unknown Mexico (New York: Scribners, 1902), and Wendell C. Bennett and Robert Zingg's The Tarahumara (Chicago: University of Chicago, 1935)—and others cited in the Co-Evolution story—I added pharmacological material from C. Pennington's The Tarahumara of Mexico (Salt Lake City: University of Utah, 1963), and came up with rare commentary such as John A. White's "Tarahumaris Indians of Mexico are Champion Runners" (The American Indian, Tulsa, Aug. 1929, p. 2).

CHAPTER EIGHT

My overview here but introduces the book about Indian runners on the white man's tracks which is waiting to be written. It will reveal hidden history about Indian and white relations in this century as well as give forgotten athletes their rightful place in sports history. The opening quote is from Parsons (PIR p. 821). The Micmac story is in Silas Rand's Legends of the Micmacs (New York: Longmans, Green, 1894). Tom Longboat's career was chronicled in a fifteen page file of news clippings, biographical chronologies and documentation from Woodland Indian Cultural Educational Centre of Brantford, Ontario; courtesy of Mrs. Lillian Montour (personal communication, 9 Feb. 1981). For the Cariisle experience I used Jack Newcombe's The Best of the Athletic Boys (New York: Doubleday, 1975) and biographical sketches of Tewanima and Thorpe from Frederick J. Dockstater's Great North American Indians (New York: Van Nostrand, 1977). Mary Coolidge's The Rain-Makers (Boston: Houghton Mifflin, 1929) contains details of lesser known 20th century Indian track stars, and Thomas Buckley located the Grants Pass data.

William Simmons of U.C. Berkeley alerted me to the exciting profile of Ellison Brown in Jerry Nason's "Born To Run" (Yankee, April 1981) and, incidentally, showed me where David Maybury-Lewis had joined the Sherente in their log-races. The brief Tarahumara entry into the white man's arena is from numerous sources, notably Enrique Hank Lopez' "The Shoeless Mexicans vs. the Flying Finn" (American Heritage, V. 25, N. 3) and Michael Jenkinson's "The Glory of the Long Distance Runner" (Natural History, Jan. 1972).

For physiological material on Indian runners I used David Costill, et al.'s "Determinants of Marathon Running Success" and Piero Aghemo, et al.'s "Maximal Aerobic Power in Primitive Indians," both in (Internationale Zettschrift fur Angewandte Physiologie . . . Band 29, Heft 3. 1971), Bruno Balke and Clyde Snow's "Anthropological and Physiological Observations on Tarahumara Endurance Runners" (American Journal of Physical Anthro., V. 23, 1965), Henry C. Fleming's "Medical Observations on the Zuni Indians" (New York: Museum of American Indian Contrib., 1924), and "Race for Gold" (Boston: WGBH transcript, NOVA T.V. show, 1979, by Paula S. Apsell).

Joe Sando's data from Jemez and Bertram Gabriel's Sports Illustrated piece launched me into contemporary Indian running; then Edward Abbey's "Casting Shadows in the Desert" (Running, Nov.-Dec. 1980), Robert Barnett's "The New American Footrace" (The Runner, Dec. 1980), the Oakland Intertribal Friendship House's documentation on the 500-mile Spiritual Run, and Ward Churchill's "General Assessment: 1978 All Indian Long Distance Runner's Training Camp, Boulder, 1979," helped complete the picture. The problems and promise of today's young Indian runners, as compassionately expressed to me by Mike Kakuska, former recreation coordinator at Zuni Pueblo, deserve to be the subject of future writings.

Spider Woman's story is in Alexander M. Stephen's "Hopi Tales" (Journal of American Folklore, V. 42, 1929, p. 37) while the Navajo chant is a section of the Mountain Chant recorded in 1946 and 1947 for Santa Fe's Museum of Navajo Ceremonial Art (Astrov, 1950, p. 52).

Photograph and Illustration Credits

(Photographs unless otherwise noted. Complete book and magazine article references cited in "Notes on Sources.")

Karl Kernberger, p. 1, 53, 54, 57, 59, 60, 65, 78-79, 102-103, 124, 130, 133, 147, 150-151, 164-165, 169(bottom), 173(bottom), 175, 190, and cover background.

Courtesy of Denver Public Library, Western History Collections, p. 2.

David Noble, p. 8.

Courtesy of Southwest Museum, Los Angeles: p. 10, 49(top), 72-73, 101, 118, 119, 128.

Illustration from Bourke's *Medicine Men of the Apache*, p. 13.

Illustration from Poma de Ayala's *Nuevos Coronicos y Buen Cobierno*, p. 19.

Courtesy of California Academy of Sciences, painting by Awa Tsireh, p. 21.

Courtesy of Smithsonian Institution: p. 24-25, 46, 69, 75; illustration, p. 85.

Courtesy of Museum of the American Indian, Heye Foundation: Emery Kopta, p. 30; painting by Arlo Nuvayouma, p. 33; p. 104, 116, 186, 193, 205.

Sam Bingham, p. 36, 76.

Illustrations from Parson's *Taos Pueblo*, p. 39; *The Social Organization of the Tewa of New Mexico*, p. 51.

Courtesy of Colorado Historical Society, p. 44.

Illustrations from Opler's "The Jicarilla Apache Ceremonial Relay Race," p. 48(top), 49(bottom).

Courtesy of American Museum of Natural History, p. 48(bottom).

Illustration by George Catlin, from Mooney's "The Cherokee Ball Play," p. 67.

Courtesy of Museum of New Mexico: Emil Bibo, p. 80; p. 108-109; (from School of the American Research Collection, p. 113 and painting by LeRoy Kewanyema, p. 148); p. 136, 155(bottom); 196, 201.

Illustration from Hoffman's "Remarks on Ojibwa Ball Play," p. 83, 99.

Courtesy of Arizona State Museum, p. 88, 122(bottom).

Courtesy of American Philosophical Society, painting, p. 92.

Curt Nimuendajú p. 94-95; illustration from *The Eastern Timbira*, p. 96(top); p. 96 (bottom).

Dolores Newton, p. 97, 98.

Illustration from Stevenson's "Zuni Games," p. 107.

Illustration from Kroeber's *Zuni Kin and Clan*, p. 111.

Illustration from Underhill's *The Papago Indians of Arizona and their Relatives, the Pima*, p. 121.

Illustration redrawn from Drucker's *Culture Element Distribution*, p. 122(top).

Illustration redrawn from Navajo sandpainting: House of Jalth-Hasteen (Toad Man) of Hail Chant. mary C. Weelwright's *Hail Chant and Water Chant*, (New Mexico: Museum of Navajo Ceremonial Art, 1946), p. 131.

Leonard McCombe, *Navajo Means People*, (Cambridge: Harvard University Press, 1951), p. 141.

Illustration from Colton's *Hopi Kachina Dolls*, p. 154, 173(top).

Courtesy of Museum of Northern Arizona, p. 155(top).

Courtesy of Field Museum of Natural History, p. 156(top), 156(bottom), 157.

Illustration from Stephen's *Hopi Journal*, p. 160.

Joseph Mora (courtesy of John R. Wilson), p. 162.

Wendell C. Bennett and Robert Zingg (courtesy of Dr. J. Charles Kelley), p. 168.

Fr. Luis Verplancken, S.J., p. 169(top), 170.

Courtesy of Woodland Indian Cultural Educational Centre, Brantford, Ontario: Roy Mitchell, p. 176.

Courtesy of University of Oklahoma Library: Western History Collections, p. 180.

Courtesy of *Four Winds Magazine*, from Cumberland County Historical Society, p. 181.

World Wide Photos, Inc., p. 184-185.

Joe Sando, p. 189.

All other photos by the author.

Index

Hopi Basket Dance Racers, 1919.

206

MARTHA PEARSON

PETER NABOKOV is a research associate of the Museum of the American Indian, Heye Foundation. His books include *Two Leggings: The Making of a Crow Warrior, Tijerina and The Courthouse Raid,* and *Native American Testimony,* an anthology of Indian and white relations as seen through Indian eyes. In collaboration with Bob Easton he is preparing the first major survey of American Indian architectural traditions, to be published by Oxford University Press in 1982. He is a PhD candidate in anthropology at the University of California at Berkeley. For the past twenty-four years, Peter Nabokov has lived and in various capacities worked on the Souix, Navajo, Crow, Penobscot and Alabama-Coushatta reservations.